Crocheted
Cushions

DEDICATION

For my grandmother Caroline Edith Mary Samworth – known to me as 'Nana May' – who patiently taught me to crochet when I was a child, and for my daughter Elisabeth Grace Cockrell – known to everyone as 'Lillie' – who is the only one of my children to learn and enjoy this versatile craft.

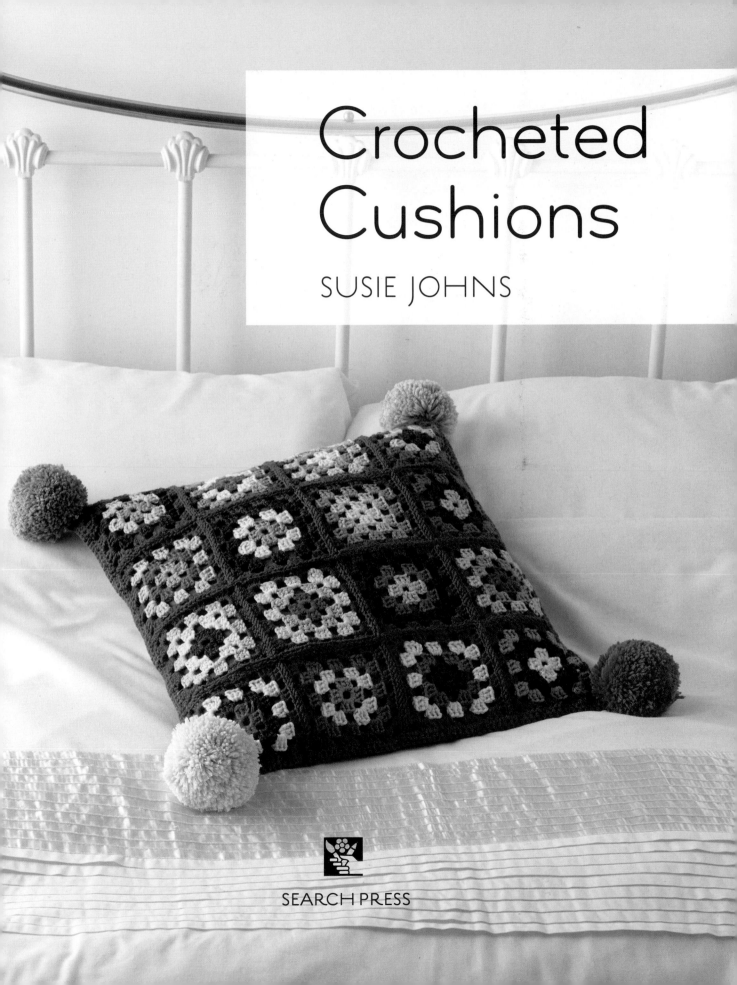

Crocheted Cushions

SUSIE JOHNS

SEARCH PRESS

First published in 2014

Search Press Limited
Wellwood, North Farm Road,
Tunbridge Wells, Kent TN2 3DR

Suppliers
If you have difficulty in obtaining any of the materials and
equipment mentioned in this book, then please visit the Search
Press website for details of suppliers:
www.searchpress.com

You are invited to visit the author's website:
www.susieatthecircus.typepad.com

Please note:
Standard UK crochet terms have been
used throughout this book. UK–US
crochet conversions are given on page
126 or, alternatively, please see the US
edition of this title, *Crocheted Pillows:*
ISBN: 978 1 78221 103 7

Printed in China

Preface

My grandmother and mother taught me to crochet when I was just eight years old. We made a patchwork blanket together, and the granny square still remains one of my favourite crochet patterns. When I was asked to write a book on crocheted cushions, the granny square was my starting point – you will find two cushions using granny square motifs (see pages 54–57 and 86–89) – but there are lots of other stitch patterns and styles as well. In fact, there are twenty-six different cushion designs within these pages. I have tried to introduce variations in colour, texture, shape and size, while also trying to ensure that every cushion is easy to make, even if you are relatively new to crochet.

It was my aim to design a cushion to suit every type of situation. There are cushions here for every room in the house: the kitchen, dining room, sitting room, bedroom, nursery, study, conservatory, and maybe even the bathroom. You can even crochet cushions for the garden, the car, caravan, boat or beach hut – not forgetting to make a few to take on picnics or fishing trips. You may wish to crochet a cushion or two for yourself but any of the cushions in this book would make a lovely gift for someone you care about. Some of the cushions are sophisticated enough for a chic modern apartment or classic, elegant interior while others are unashamedly 'silly': a novelty owl cushion (see pages 26–29), for example, and one with a spooky spider's web (see pages 34–37).

I love bright colours, and I am an inveterate hoarder, so I have included two very colourful cushions that are perfect for using up yarn scraps (see pages 50–53 and 62–65). Of course, colour is a matter of taste but that is where your own creativity comes in: you can choose your own palette of colours for any of the cushions in this book, to suit your own tastes and the colour themes in your home. Crochet and knitting are enjoying a big revival and there is plenty of lovely yarn out there from which you can make your choices, so get carried away with crocheting cushions!

Contents

Introduction

Crochet comes from a bygone age, when cushion covers would be hand-made, not mass-produced. But that doesn't mean a crocheted cushion has to be old-fashioned: there are twenty-six gorgeous, contemporary designs to choose from in this book. Crocheting cushion covers is easy and the results can be sophisticated, classy, quirky, subtle, eye-catching or just plain charming. Crochet is also very versatile. Many cushion covers can be made in one piece, without too many seams and with very little finishing off to do. You can also adapt patterns quite easily to suit your decor, your lifestyle and your budget, by using your own colour palette or by substituting your own choice of yarns – even using up oddments left over from previous projects.

It is assumed that you already know the basics of crochet or that you can find this information from another source. You may, however, have never made a cushion before, so you will find lots of general advice and information in the following few pages, including how to make your own cushion pads. While we are on the subject, when choosing or making a cushion pad it is important to decide whether you want your finished cushion to be firm and supportive – especially important for a bolster or a long rectangular cushion that can be used as a back support – or soft and supple, so that you can sink into it. For a firm result, choose a pad that is slightly larger than the finished cushion cover – but not too large, or it may distort the cover and stretch it out of shape. For a softer result, choose a pad that fits the cover exactly but is not over-stuffed with filling. Guidance is given with each project.

Each pattern is clearly set out and contains a list of all the tools and materials you will need. Hook sizes are given in metric, with US and old UK sizes also provided. Try to use the recommended yarn or something as close as possible – follow the yarn notes given with each project for advice on substitution. If you have to substitute a different yarn, you are advised to make a tension sample and measure this against the tension given for that project: read the notes on tension on page 126, where you will also find a list of abbreviations used in the patterns, which are written using UK crochet terms.

With all this at your fingertips, in next to no time – and with very little effort – you can produce a batch of beautiful cushions to accessorise your home. Then, when visitors compliment your beautiful home furnishings, you can proudly say, "I made them myself".

Materials

Crochet is a simple craft that requires few tools and materials. If you are a keen crocheter, you will already have a selection of hooks and maybe even a basket of yarn left over from other projects. That's really all you need to get started. Most people have scissors and measuring tools; on these pages, there are some suggestions for other items you will find useful.

Yarns

Yarns are classified by weight. While most of the cushion covers in this book have been made using DK or double-knitting (8-ply) yarns, fine fingering (4-ply) yarns have been used for some of the smaller cushions and aran (worsted) yarn for some of the larger ones. Yarns are also made up of different fibres, both natural and man-made. As a general rule, I prefer to use natural fibres, as these are soft on the hands when crocheting and they produce good results: wool and wool-blend yarns, especially those containing alpaca or cashmere, are warm, soft and cosy; while cotton yarns are crisp and cool, with good stitch definition. Where I wanted really bright colours, however, I used acrylic yarns for their vibrancy and colour range. Look carefully at the ball band when buying yarn: check the fibre content and the washing instructions. Natural yarns tend to be a little more expensive than those made of synthetic fibres and sometimes require hand washing. If the specified yarn for any of the patterns in this book is not available, or you decide to substitute another, similar yarn, you will need to check the yarn length on the ball band, to make sure you have enough to complete the project. You will also need to check the tension given for the pattern (see page 126 for guidance) before proceeding.

Hooks

Various different hook sizes have been used to make the crocheted cushions in this book and they have been chosen in order to produce a particular result. Sometimes a different sized hook from the one recommended by the manufacturers has been used, usually in order to produce a firm fabric. Whichever cushion you choose to make, if you want it to end up the same size as the one shown in the picture, it is important to check your tension so that you don't end up with a cover that is too big or too small to fit the size of cushion pad specified.

Buttons and zips

Buttons provide not only an effective fastening but an attractive design detail – and there are so many shapes, sizes and colours, you'll be spoilt for choice. Zips are also useful for covers you wish to remove. The type of zip you use will depend on the size and weight of the cushion: a lightweight zip is fine for a small cushion but for a larger, heavier cushion a heavier zip, such as the metal zip shown on page 101, might be preferable.

Other equipment

A small pair of scissors will be necessary for snipping yarn ends. If you intend to make your own cushion pads, you will also need a good pair of dressmaking shears for cutting fabrics, and a tape measure.

Pins, needles and threads

A blunt tapestry needle is useful for darning in yarn ends and for sewing seams or joining components. It can also be useful for threading ribbon through eyelet holes, though you may prefer to use a bodkin or a safety pin for this. Safety pins can also be used to pin pieces of crocheted fabric together prior to sewing; of course you can also use straight pins for this, but it is advisable to choose ones with glass heads as these are easier to see and less likely to be left behind, buried in the fabric. You will also need a sewing needle and thread for stitching buttons and zips in place.

Trimmings

Bobble braid has been used to trim the cushions on pages 50–53 and velvet ribbon has been threaded through rows of eyelet holes on pages 106–109. There is a huge range of trimmings to choose from, so hunt around in haberdashery shops and online to find those perfect finishing touches.

Techniques

Making cushion pads

You can buy ready-made cushion pads in a range of sizes and shapes, and with different fillings, such as feathers, polyester fiberfill, foam chips and polystyrene beads. If you need a pad that does not conform to the commonly available sizes, however, you can make your own quite easily. Use a closely woven, medium-weight fabric such as cotton cambric, calico or ticking.

Square or rectangle

1 Cut two pieces of fabric, 1cm (½in) larger all round than the size you want your finished cushion pad to be. Place the two pieces right sides together, and pin and tack together along all four edges.

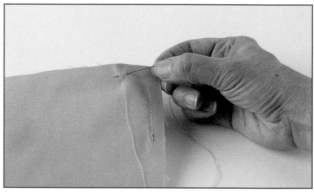

2 Using hand backstitch or your sewing machine, sew the pieces together, 1cm (½in) from the edge, leaving a gap in your stitching of 6–8cm (2½–3in). If you are sewing a rectangle, leave the gap on one of the shorter edges. Fasten off the thread.

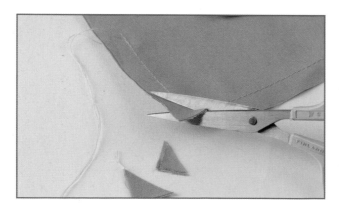

3 Cut off the four corners, being careful not to snip too close to the stitching – this will give you sharp, neat corners when you turn your fabric the right way out.

4 Using the hole you left in the stitching, turn the cover right sides out and then press.

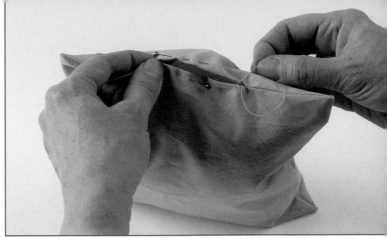

5 Fill the cushion pad with your chosen stuffing. Push the stuffing right into the corners but do not overfill the pad.

6 Fold in the raw edges on the opening by 1cm (½in) and pin them in place. Slip stitch the folded edges together.

Circle

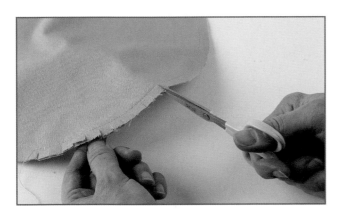

Cut two circles of fabric with a diameter 2cm (¾in) larger than you want the finished pad to be. Pin and tack the two circles together, right sides facing. Using hand backstitch or your sewing machine, sew the pieces together, 1cm (½in) from the edge, leaving a gap in your stitching of 6–8cm (2½–3in). Fasten off the thread. Carefully snip small incisions about 1cm (½in) apart all the way round the edge of the cushion pad. Turn the cushion pad right sides out. Stuff it, then fold the raw edges of the opening under, pin in place, and slipstitch the folded edges together.

Ball

1 Use the template and size guide on pages 126 and 127 to create eight identical pieces of fabric.

2 Sew two pieces together lengthwise – the pieces will curve as you join them. Continue to join the segments together – the ball shape will begin to form as you do this – then finally, sew the edges between the first and last pieces together, leaving a 6–8cm (2½–3in) gap in the centre of the seam. Trim away excess fabric at the ends of the seams, where all the points meet, to reduce bulk. Turn the cushion pad right sides out and fill it with stuffing. Fold the raw edges of the opening under, pin in place, then slipstitch the gap closed.

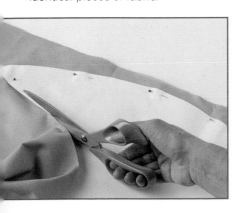

Seams

Joining pieces of crochet together needs to be done as neatly as possible as untidy seams will spoil the appearance of your finished cushion. There are several methods of joining pieces of crochet for a neat result. In the four examples given, contrasting yarns have been used to show the joins as clearly as possible.

Creating a backstitch seam

This is one of the neatest methods for joining two edges of row-ends together. Two edges, even when they are made up of the same number of rows, can be slightly tighter or looser than each other, so to make sure the seam is even it is a good idea to pin together the edges to be joined, before stitching.

1 Place the two pieces on top of one another, right sides together. Place pins at intervals to hold the edges in place. Thread a blunt tapestry needle with a long length of yarn. Secure the yarn end to the fabric and bring it up through the back of both pieces on the right hand edge. Working from right to left, push the needle down through both layers, then bring it back up about 5mm (¼in) to the left.

2 Pull the needle and yarn right the way through. Insert the needle back through the pieces, next to the first stitch, and then bring it back up through both layers about 5mm (¼in) to the left of the completed stitch.

3 Repeat steps 1 and 2, taking the needle about 5mm (¼in) or two rows to the left each time, and one row back. Fasten off the yarn securely and weave in the yarn end neatly.

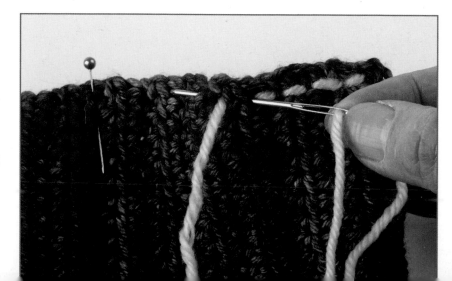

Oversewing a seam

This is more suitable for joining the tops of rows, or foundation edges, than for joining row ends. The method creates a slight ridge so it is better for joining the back and front of a cushion cover than for piecing squares together to make a patchwork.

1 Place the two edges to be joined together. If it helps, place pins at intervals to hold the edges in place.

2 Thread a blunt tapestry needle with yarn – this will usually be the tail of yarn left after fastening off, which will still be attached to the work. If the two edges are different colours, choose one of these. Working from right to left, take the needle from the back, through the first stitch on one edge, then through the corresponding stitch on the other edge.

3 Take the needle over the edge to the back again, then through the next pair of stitches.

4 Repeat this to the end of the seam. Fasten off the yarn securely and weave in the yarn end neatly.

Creating a flat seam

Once again, this method is better for joining two rows of stitches, rather than row ends, and is particularly useful for joining squares together, as in Granny (pages 54–57) and Patch (pages 86–89).

1 Thread a tapestry needle with yarn and pass it through one loop only of the end stitch on the back piece, then one loop of the corresponding stitch on the front piece.

2 Take the needle through the next stitch to the left, from the front, then back through the starting stitch.

3 Now take it through the next stitch to the left on the back piece, back through the last stitch worked on the front piece, and pull through to the front. Thread the needle through the next stitch to the left on the front, then back through the last stitch worked on the back.

4 Repeat the sequence in step 3 weaving in and out of the stitches from back to front, and back again. Keep the stitches loose, then, every few stitches, pull on the yarn to tighten them slightly and to draw the two edges together. Do not pull too tightly or the edge will become puckered. Fasten off when you reach the end.

Creating a double crochet seam

This seam can be used to join any two edges together and it forms a decorative ridge that looks neat when viewed from both the front and the back. It can be used to create a border and can be worked in a matching or contrasting yarn.

1 Place the two pieces to be joined on top of one another, right sides out. Place pins at intervals, if necessary, to hold the edges together. Join the yarn to the first stitch, then insert the hook from front to back through one loop only of the first stitch on both edges.

2 Wrap the yarn over the hook and draw the yarn through to the front. Wrap the yarn around the hook again and draw it through both loops on the hook, to complete the first double crochet stitch.

3 Repeat along the edge, inserting the hook through one loop only of each corresponding pair of stitches on both pieces. When you reach the end, cut the yarn, fasten off and weave in the yarn tail.

Fastenings

If you want to be able to remove the cushion cover, it is a good idea to include some kind of fastening, or simply to leave an opening, with an overlap to help keep the cushion pad in place. Several of the cushions in this book have an overlap, such as Tartan (pages 94–97), while others make a feature of decorative buttons, such as Spike (pages 70–73). Snail (pages 98–101) features a central zip fastening on the back, and you can choose to add a zip to many of the other cushions, if you like, placing it on the back of the cushion or in one of the side seams, if you prefer.

Adding a zip

A zip can be placed in a side seam or where two edges meet on the back of a cushion cover, which might be in the centre or towards one edge. Choose a zip that is slightly shorter – about 2–3cm (¾–1¼in) shorter for a medium-sized cushion – than the edges to be joined. You can decide how much the fabric overlaps the teeth: cover the teeth if you want to hide the zip, or attach it further back if you want to make a feature of the zip.

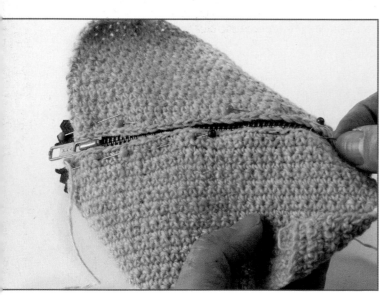

1 Place the edge of one of the pieces to be joined right side up along the centre of the zip and pin in place. Pin the second piece along the other edge, lining up the ends of the crocheted fabric. Thread a sewing needle with thread to match the yarn and, working from the right side, stitch through both the crocheted fabric and the fabric of the zip, in backstitch, close to the edge of the teeth.

2 Turn the work over and slipstitch the edges of the zip to the crocheted fabric on either side. When you have finished, fold back the fabric at the ends of the zip and stitch in place, so that it will be clear of the cushion seams.

Adding buttons

Button fastenings can be decorative as well as practical. Some of the cushions in this book feature button fastenings, but you can always add your own to a cushion with an overlap by leaving gaps in the last or second-to-last row in the pattern, or by adding an edging that incorporates button loops.

1 Stitch the cushion seams as indicated in the pattern. Use safety pins to mark the placement of each button, in line with the buttonholes or loops.

2 Choose buttons that will fit easily through the buttonholes but that are not so small that they come undone easily, and sew them in place using thread that matches or contrasts with the crocheted fabric.

Covering a button

Instructions are given on page 60 for crocheting a button cover. You can make covered buttons using your own choice of yarn and the appropriate sized hook. Choose a button large enough to accommodate the cover when it is gathered up. You can use a button with holes or one with a shank.

1 Crochet the button cover, fasten off and leave a tail of yarn. Thread this tail into a blunt needle and run the needle in and out of the stitches on the edge of the disc.

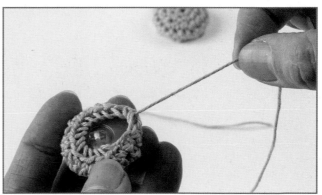

2 Place the crocheted disc face down and place a button inside. Pull up the yarn end to gather the edge of the cover and enclose the button, then fasten off securely.

The cushions

Flowers

Children will find this small-scale cushion just right for dolls and teddies – and it would also look charming as part of a group of larger cushions in a country kitchen, in a conservatory or on a child-sized garden chair.

CUSHION PATTERN

The main part of the cushion is worked in a simple variation of double crochet, where pairs of double crochet stitches are linked, producing an all-over ridged texture. The flowers and leaves are made separately, in the round, and stitched in place. The two sides of the cushion cover are joined with a double crochet seam (see page 17) in a contrasting colour, with an extra round of double crochet creating a narrow border.

Tension

21 sts and 26 rows to 10cm (4in) measured over linked double crochet pattern, using 3.50mm (US E/4, UK 9) hook and recommended yarn.

Front

Foundation chain: with 3.50mm (US E/4, UK 9) hook and yarn A, make 40 ch.

Foundation row: 1 dc in 2nd ch from hook, *dc2tog, inserting hook into same ch as last st and into next ch; rep from * to end; turn (39 sts).

Row 1: 1 ch (does not count as a st), 1 dc in 1st st, *dc2tog, inserting hook into same st and into next st; rep from * to end; turn.

Rep row 1 47 times.

Cut yarn and fasten off.

Back

Follow instructions for Front but use yarn B.

Leaf (make three)

Foundation chain: with 3.50mm (US E/4, UK 9) hook and yarn C, make 23 ch.

Round 1: 1 dc in 2nd ch from hook, 1 dc in each of next 9 ch, 1 htr in next ch, 1 tr in each of next 2 ch, 1 dtr in each of next 4 ch, 1 tr in each of next 2 ch, 1 htr in next ch, 1 dc in last ch; do not turn but work 3 ch, then working along opposite edge of foundation chain, 1 dc in 1st ch, 1 htr in next ch, 1 tr in each of next 2 ch, 1 dtr in each of next 4 ch, 1 tr in each of next 2 ch, 1 htr in next ch, 1 dc in next ch, ss into next ch.

Cut yarn, leaving a tail, and fasten off.

Equipment

YARN:

DK (8-ply) cotton yarn, 1 x 100g (3½oz) ball each in china blue (A), greengage (B), pine green (C), pink (D) and apricot (E)

HOOK:

3.50mm (US E/4, UK 9)

CUSHION PAD:

Square, 20 x 20cm (8 x 8in)

MEASUREMENTS:

21 x 21cm (8½ x 8½in), including border

Yarn Notes

This cushion has been made using Patons 100 per cent Cotton DK, a tightly spun mercerised cotton available in a good range of vibrant colours. There are 330m (360 yds) in a 100g (3½oz) ball. A classic yarn like this is the perfect choice for crochet projects as it is firm, smooth and easy to work with, and produces excellent stitch definition.

Flower (make two in yarn D, one in yarn E)

Foundation chain: with 3.50mm (US E/4, UK 9) hook and yarn B, make 4 ch; join with a ss to 1st ch to form a ring.

Round 1: 3 ch (counts as 1 tr), 11 tr into ring; join with a ss to 3rd of 3 ch (12 sts).

Round 2: 1 ch (does not count as a st), 2 dc in same place, 2 dc in each st to end (24 sts); cut yarn B.

Round 3: join yarn D or E to any dc of previous round, (4 ch, 1 dtr in next dc, 2 dtr in next dc, 1 dtr in next dc, 4 ch, ss in next dc) six times.

Cut yarn, leaving a tail, and fasten off.

Making up and border

Pin the three leaves to the cushion Front and stitch in place using tails of yarn. Arrange flowers on top, pin in place, then stitch, using tails of yarn. Weave in any remaining yarn tails.

Place the Front and Back of the cushion together, right sides out, and join all round edges using yarn E and double crochet (see page 17), inserting the hook into one loop each of every dc on the two edges. When the seam is two-thirds complete, insert the cushion pad and continue joining the two edges; fasten off and weave in tails of yarn. Work a second round of dc, working 1 dc in each dc along straight edges and 3 dc into each of the four corner stitches.

Made separately and sewn in place in the centre of the cushion front, the leaves and flowers add a touch of texture as well as a splash of colour.

When sewing the flowers and leaves in place, leave the edges unstitched, to enhance the three-dimensional effect.

You can tell the 'right' side of the motifs: the tops of the stitches around the edge of each petal form a distinctive chain, which is not evident on the 'wrong' side.

Owl

This owl would make a comfortable companion for a child or an amusing mascot for an adult. Crocheted in DK (8-ply) wool, he is soft and cosy and the shell pattern gives the impression of a feathered breast. Use these bright, bold colours for a quirky finish, or swap them for more natural colours.

CUSHION PATTERN

This cushion is worked in an interlocking shell stitch.

Tension

21 sts and 19 rows to 10cm (4in) measured over rows of dc using 4.00mm (US G/6, UK 8) hook and the recommended yarn.

Front and Back

Foundation chain: with 4.00mm (US G/6, UK 8) hook and yarn A, make 45 ch.

Foundation round: 2 tr in 3rd ch from hook, * (miss 2 ch, 1 dc in next ch, miss 2 ch, 5 tr in next ch) six times, miss 2 ch, 1 dc in next ch, miss 2 ch, 2 tr in last ch **, do not turn but work 3 tr in other side of last ch then, working along the opposite side of the foundation ch, rep from * to **; join with ss to top of turning ch at beg of round; do not cut A but join in B.

Round 1: using B, 1 ch (does not count as a st), 1 dc in top of turning ch on previous round, (2 ch, tr5tog over next 5 sts, 2 ch, 1 dc in next st [which is centre st of 5-tr shell]) 13 times, 2 ch, tr5tog over next 5 sts, 2 ch; join with a ss in 1st dc of round, pulling yarn A through as you do so.

Round 2: using A, 3 ch (counts as 1 tr), 2 tr in same place, *(miss 2 ch, 1 dc in top of tr5tog, miss 2 ch, 5 tr in next dc) 13 times, miss 2 ch, 1 dc in top of last tr5tog, miss 2 ch, 2 tr in same place as (3 ch, 2 tr) at beg of round.

Rep rounds 1 and 2 11 times; cut yarn A and continue in B.

Round 25: 1 ch, 1 dc in turning ch of previous round, 1 dc in each of next 2 tr, (1 htr in next dc, 1 dc in each of next 5 tr) 13 times, 1 htr in next dc, 1 dc in each of last 2 tr; join with a ss to 1st dc of round.

Round 26: 1 ch, 1 dc in each st of last round (84 sts).

Rep round 26 21 times.

Cut yarn and fasten off.

Eye (make two)

Foundation round: with 4.00mm (US G/6, UK 8) hook and yarn D, make a magic ring and work 1 ch (does not count as a st), 6 dc into ring; join with a ss to 1st dc of round (6 sts).

Round 1: 1 ch, 2 dc in each dc of previous round (12 sts).

Round 2: 1 ch, 2 dc in each dc of previous round (24 sts).

EQUIPMENT

YARN:
Pure wool DK (8-ply) yarn, 1 x 50g (1¾oz) ball each in dark red (A), pale grey (B), dark teal (C) and ivory (D)

HOOK:
4.00mm (US G/6, UK 8)

CUSHION PAD:
Rectangular, 35 x 25cm (14 x 10in)

MEASUREMENTS:
35 x 25cm (14 x 10in)

Yarn Notes

This cushion has been made using Debbie Bliss Rialto DK, a classic DK (8-ply) yarn spun from extra fine merino wool, which makes it deliciously soft and luxurious. There are 105m (115 yds) in a 50g (1¾oz) ball. You could substitute any standard DK (8-ply) yarn but be sure to crochet a tension sample to ensure that your cushion ends up the right size.

Round 3: 1 ch, 1 dc in each of 1st 3 dc, (2 dc in next dc, 1 dc in each of next 3 dc) five times, 2 dc in last dc; join with a ss to 1st dc of round (30 sts).

Round 4: 1 ch, 1 dc in each dc of previous round; cut yarn D and join in C.

Round 5: 1 ch, 1 dc in each of 1st 4 dc, (2 dc in next dc, 1 dc in each of next 4 dc) five times, 2 dc in last dc; join with a ss to 1st dc of round (36 sts).

Cut yarn, leaving a long tail, and fasten off.

Eye centre (make two)

Foundation round: with 4.00mm hook (US G/6, UK 8) and yarn C, make a magic ring and work 1 ch (does not count as a st), 6 dc into ring; join with a ss to 1st dc of round (6 sts).

Round 1: 1 ch, 2 dc in each dc of previous round (12 sts).

Cut yarn, leaving a long tail, and fasten off.

Eyebrow (make two)

With 4.00mm (US G/6, UK 8) hook and yarn A, make 12 ch.

Cut yarn, leaving a tail, and fasten off.

Beak

Foundation row: with 4.00mm (US G/6, UK 8) hook and yarn D, make 2 ch, 3 dc in 2nd ch from hook; turn.

Row 1: 2 dc in 1st dc, 1 dc in 2nd dc, 2 dc in 3rd dc; turn (5 sts).

Row 2: 1 ch, 1 dc in each dc of previous row.

Row 3: 2 dc in 1st dc, 1 dc in each of next 3 dc, 2 dc in last dc; turn (7 sts).

Row 4: 1 ch, 1 dc in each dc of previous row.

Row 5: 2 dc in 1st dc, 1 dc in each of next 5 dc, 2 dc in last dc; turn (9 sts).

Row 6: 1 ch, 1 dc in each dc of previous row.

Row 7: as row 6.

Cut yarn, leaving a tail, and fasten off.

Making up

Pin the eyes in place on the front of the cushion cover and, using yarn tails, stitch in place, oversewing edges to main fabric (see top tip box). Stitch eye centres in place. Stitch beak in place centrally, below the eyes. Stitch eyebrows in place above eyes. Place the cushion pad inside the cover and join top seam by stitching or with a double crochet seam. Thread a tapestry needle with a length of yarn B and stitch across each of the top corners, in backstitch.

TOP TIP

Pin the eyes and eyebrows in place before stitching; this will allow for repositioning, so that you can alter the owl's expression. Thread the yarn tail into a blunt tapestry needle and oversew or slipstitch the stitch loops to the background fabric.

This shell stitch pattern, worked in two contrasting colours, has been chosen to suggest feathers.

The eyes, eyebrows and beak are made separately and stitched in place. Keep your stitches small, to give a neat appearance and to ensure that these components are firmly secured.

Try to choose a cushion pad that fits the owl cover exactly. It is best not to overstuff your owl, as you will want him to be soft, squishy and cuddly. You will also need to push down the two upper corners of the cushion pad, in order to stitch across the cover and form triangular 'ears'.

Ball

Made from a cotton jersey yarn, this large, plump sphere is practical as well as stylish and very satisfying to make. Filled with polystyrene beads, it is lightweight but very sturdy and makes an excellent floor cushion or footstool for a nursery, bedroom or living room.

CUSHION PATTERN

This cushion is worked in rounds of double crochet, inserting the hook into the back loop only of every stitch, which creates a subtle ridged effect. You will need to work increases on every other round to create the circular shape.

Tension

9 sts and 8 rows to 10cm (4in) measured over rows of dc using 8.00mm (US L/11, UK 0) hook and the recommended yarn.

Side 1

Foundation round: with 8.00mm (US L/11, UK 0) hook and yarn A, make a magic ring and work 1 ch, 6 dc in ring; join with a ss to 1st dc of round.

> ### Note:
> Insert hook into back loop only of each stitch throughout.

Round 1: 1 ch (does not count as a stitch), 2 dc in each dc of previous round; join with a ss to 1st dc of round (12 sts).

Round 2: 1 ch, 2 dc in each dc of previous round; join with a ss to 1st dc of round (24 sts).

Round 3: 1 ch, 1 dc in 1st dc, 2 dc in next dc, (1 dc in next dc, 2 dc in next dc) 11 times; join with a ss to 1st dc of round (36 sts).

Round 4: 1 ch, 1 dc in 1st dc, 1 dc in next dc, 2 dc in next dc, (1 dc in each of next 2 dc, 2 dc in next dc) 11 times; join with a ss to 1st dc of round (48 sts).

Round 5: 1 ch, 1 dc in each dc of previous round; join with a ss to 1st dc of round.

Round 6: 1 ch, 1 dc in 1st dc, 1 dc in each of next 2 dc, 2 dc in next dc, (1 dc in each of next 3 dc, 2 dc in next dc) 11 times; join with a ss to 1st dc of round (60 sts).

Round 7: 1 ch, 1 dc in each dc of previous round; join with a ss to 1st dc of round.

Round 8: 1 ch, 1 dc in 1st dc, 1 dc in each of next 3 dc, 2 dc in next dc, (1 dc in each of next 4 dc, 2 dc in next dc) 11 times; join with a ss to 1st dc of round (72 sts).

Round 9: 1 ch, 1 dc in each dc of previous round; join with a ss to 1st dc of round.

Round 10: 1 ch, 1 dc in 1st dc, 1 dc in each of next 4 dc, 2 dc in next dc, (1 dc in each of next 5 dc, 2 dc in next dc) 11 times; join with a ss to 1st dc of round (84 sts).

EQUIPMENT

YARN:
Stretch jersey yarn, 120m (131 yds) in fuchsia (A) and in pink (B)

HOOK:
8.00mm (US L/11, UK 0)

CUSHION PAD:
Ball, 50cm (20in) diameter filled with polystyrene beads

MEASUREMENTS:
50cm (20in) in diameter

Yarn Notes

This cushion has been made using Hoooked Zpagetti from DMC, a unique yarn made from offcuts of stretchy 98 per cent cotton fabrics. There are 120m (131 yds) in a cone. Though the yarn is thick, it is smooth and easy to work with. If you cannot find this or a similar yarn to buy, why not make your own from recycled t-shirts? Cut off the sleeves, neckband and hem and then, beginning at the lower edge, cut a strip about 3cm (1¼in) wide all round; when you reach the starting point, do not cut off the strip but continue cutting around the t-shirt in a spiral so that you produce one continuous strip. You will need a number of t-shirts to create enough yarn to crochet this cushion, so have a clearout or try jumble sales and car boot sales for cheap t-shirts, leggings and other garments made from similar stretch jersey fabrics.

Round 11: 1 ch, 1 dc in each dc of previous round; join with a ss to 1st dc of round.

Round 12: 1 ch, 1 dc in 1st dc, 1 dc in each of next 5 dc, 2 dc in next dc, (1 dc in each of next 6 dc, 2 dc in next dc) 11 times; join with a ss to 1st dc of round (96 sts).

Round 13: 1 ch, 1 dc in each dc of previous round; join with a ss to 1st dc of round.

Round 14: 1 ch, 1 dc in 1st dc, 1 dc in each of next 6 dc, 2 dc in next dc, (1 dc in each of next 7 dc, 2 dc in next dc) 11 times; join with a ss to 1st dc of round (108 sts).

Round 15: 1 ch, 1 dc in each dc of previous round; join with a ss to 1st dc of round.

Round 16: 1 ch, 1 dc in 1st dc, 1 dc in each of next 7 dc, 2 dc in next dc, (1 dc in each of next 8 dc, 2 dc in next dc) 11 times; join with a ss to 1st dc of round (120 sts).

Round 17: 1 ch, 1 dc in each dc of previous round; join with a ss to 1st dc of round.

Rep round 17 six times more; cut yarn and fasten off.

Side 2

Make Side 2 following instructions for Side 1 but using yarn B; do not cut yarn at end of last round.

Making up

Place the two pieces together, right sides out, lining up edges. Join, stitch by stitch, with dc (see page 17), inserting the hook into one loop only on both edges. When seam is two-thirds complete, insert the cushion pad and continue joining the two edges; fasten off and weave in tails of yarn.

Although the cushion pad is a sphere, when the cushion is placed on a flat surface the filling settles, creating a slightly flattened profile.

The cushion cover is made in two halves which are then joined with a double-crochet seam. The seam forms an attractive ridge around the middle of the cushion.

The rounds of double crochet are worked into the back loops of the stitches of the previous round; the unworked front loops create distinct concentric circles on the surface of the fabric.

Cobweb

Make a plain round cushion cover from a luxury yarn woven with wisps of metallic thread, then add a delicate spider's web with glass beads twinkling like drops of dew.

CUSHION PATTERN

The main part of this cushion is worked in rounds of double crochet and half treble; the web is worked separately, also in the round, using chains, trebles and double trebles to create a mesh, then joined to the top of the cushion in the last round.

Tension

20 sts and 9 rows to 10cm (4in) measured over rows of htr using 3.50mm (US E/4, UK 9) hook and yarn A.

Top

Foundation round: using 3.50mm (US E/4, UK 9) hook and yarn A, make a magic ring and work 1 ch (does not count as a st), 6 dc into ring; join with a ss in 1st dc of round (6 sts).

Round 1: 1 ch, 2 dc in each dc of previous round; join with a ss in 1st dc of round (12 sts).

Round 2: 1 ch, 2 dc in each dc of previous round; join with a ss in 1st dc of round (24 sts).

Round 3: 1 ch, 1 dc in each dc of previous round; join with a ss in 1st dc of round.

Round 4: 1 ch, 1 dc in 1st st, 2 dc in next st, (1 dc in next st, 2 dc in next st) 11 times; join with a ss to 1st dc of round (36 sts).

Round 5: 1 ch, 1 dc in each dc of previous round; join with a ss in 1st dc of round.

Round 6: 1 ch, 1 dc in 1st st, 1 dc in next st, 2 dc in next st, (1 dc in each of next 2 sts, 2 dc in next st) 11 times; join with a ss in 1st dc of round (48 sts).

Round 7: 1 ch, 1 dc in each dc of previous round; join with a ss in 1st dc of round.

Round 8: 1 ch, 1 dc in 1st st, 1 dc in each of next 2 sts, 2 dc in next st, (1 dc in each of next 3 sts, 2 dc in next st) 11 times; join with a ss in 1st dc of round (60 sts).

Round 9: 2 ch (counts as 1 htr), 1 htr in next dc, 1 htr in each dc to end of round; join with a ss in 1st htr of round.

Round 10: 1 ch, 1 dc in 1st st, 1 dc in each of next 3 sts, 2 dc in next st, (1 dc in each of next 4 sts, 2 dc in next st) 11 times; join with a ss in 1st dc of round (72 sts).

Round 11: 2 ch, 1 htr in next dc, 1 htr in each dc to end of round; join with a ss in 1st htr of round.

Round 12: 1 ch, 1 dc in 1st st, 1 dc in each of next 4 sts, 2 dc in next st, (1 dc in each of next 5 sts, 2 dc in next st) 11 times; join with a ss in 1st dc of round (84 sts).

Round 13: 2 ch, 1 htr in next dc, 1 htr in each dc to end of round; join with a ss in 1st htr of round.

Round 14: 1 ch, 1 dc in 1st st, 1 dc in each of next 5 sts, 2 dc in next st, (1 dc in each of next 6 sts, 2 dc in next st) 11 times; join with a ss in 1st dc of round (96 sts).

Round 15: 2 ch, 1 htr in next dc, 1 htr in each dc to end of round; join with a ss in 1st htr of round.

Round 16: 1 ch, 1 dc in 1st st, 1 dc in each of next 6 sts, 2 dc in next st, (1 dc in each of next 7 sts, 2 dc in next st) 11 times; join with a ss in 1st dc of round (108 sts).

Round 17: 2 ch, 1 htr in next dc, 1 htr in each dc to end of round; join with a ss in 1st htr of round.

Round 18: 1 ch, 1 dc in 1st st, 1 dc in each of next 7 sts, 2 dc in next st, (1 dc in each of next 8 sts, 2 dc in next st) 11 times; join with a ss in 1st dc of round (120 sts).

Round 19: 2 ch, 1 htr in next dc, 1 htr in each dc to end of round; join with a ss in 1st htr of round.

Round 20: 1 ch, 1 dc in 1st st, 1 dc in each of next 8 sts, 2 dc in next st, (1 dc in each of next 9 sts, 2 dc in next st) 11 times; join with a ss in 1st dc of round (132 sts).

Round 21: 2 ch, 1 htr in next dc, 1 htr in each dc to end of round; join with a ss in 1st htr of round.

Round 22: 1 ch, 1 dc in 1st st, 1 dc in each of next 9 sts, 2 dc in next st, (1 dc in each of next 10 sts, 2 dc in next st) 11 times; join with a ss in 1st dc of round (144 sts).

Round 23: 2 ch, 1 htr in next dc, 1 htr in each dc to end of round; join with a ss in 1st htr of round.

Round 24: 1 ch, 1 dc in 1st st, 1 dc in each of next 10 sts, 2 dc in next st, (1 dc in each of next 11 sts, 2 dc in next st) 11 times; join with a ss in 1st dc of round (156 sts).

Round 25: 2 ch, 1 htr in next dc, 1 htr in each dc to end of round; join with a ss in 1st htr of round.

Round 26: 1 ch, 1 dc in 1st st, 1 dc in each of next 11 sts, 2 dc in next st, (1 dc in each of next 12 sts, 2 dc in next st) 11 times; join with a ss in 1st dc of round (168 sts).

Round 27: 2 ch, 1 htr in next dc, 1 htr in each dc to end of round; join with a ss in 1st htr of round.

Round 28: 1 ch, 1 dc in 1st st, 1 dc in each of next 12 sts, 2 dc in next st, (1 dc in each of next 13 sts, 2 dc in next st) 11 times; join with a ss in 1st dc of round (180 sts).

A spider's web superimposed on a round cushion cover makes an attractive novelty cushion. The ends of each 'spoke' of the web are attached on the last round, so there is no sewing involved, and the main part of the web remains separate from the surface of the cushion.

Round 29: 2 ch, 1 htr in next dc, 1 htr in each dc to end of round; join with a ss in 1st htr of round.

Round 30: 1 ch, 1 dc in 1st st, 1 dc in each of next 13 sts, 2 dc in next st, (1 dc in each of next 14 sts, 2 dc in next st) 11 times; join with a ss in 1st dc of round (192 sts).

Round 31: 2 ch, 1 htr in next dc, 1 htr in each dc to end of round; join with a ss in 1st htr of round.

Round 32: 1 ch, 1 dc in each htr of previous round; join with a ss in 1st dc of round.

Cut yarn and fasten off.

Base

Work as given for Top; do not fasten off yarn after end of round 32.

Web

Foundation chain: with 4.00mm (US G/6, UK 8) hook and yarn B, make 6 ch and join with a ss to 1st ch to form a ring.

Round 1: 6 ch (counts as 1 tr, 3 ch), (1 tr into ring, 3 ch) five times; join with ss to 3rd of 6 ch (6 spokes).

Round 2: 6 ch (counts as 1 tr, 3 ch), (1 tr into 3-ch sp, 3 ch, 1 tr into next tr, 3 ch) five times, 1 tr into 3-ch sp, 3 ch; join with ss to 3rd of 6 ch (12 spokes).

Round 3: 8 ch (counts as 1 dtr, 4 ch), (1 dtr into next tr, 4 ch) 11 times; join with ss to 4th of 8 ch.

Round 4: 10 ch (counts as 1 dtr, 6 ch), (1 dtr into next dtr, 6 ch) 11 times; join with ss to 4th of 10 ch.

Round 5: 12 ch (counts as 1 dtr, 8 ch), (1 dtr into next dtr, 8 ch) 11 times; join with ss to 4th of 12 ch.

Round 6: 14 ch (counts as 1 dtr, 10 ch), (1 dtr into next dtr, 10 ch) 11 times; join with ss to 4th of 14 ch.

Join to cushion Top.

Round 7: 16 ch (counts as 1 dtr, 12 ch), 1 dtr into next dtr, 6 ch, ss into any dc on edge of Top, ss into each of 6 ch, ss into top of dtr, 12 ch (1 dtr into next dtr, 6 ch, miss 15 dc on edge of Top, ss into next dc, ss into each of 6 ch, ss into top of dtr, 12 ch) 10 times, 1 dtr into 4th of 14 ch, 6 ch, miss 15 dc on edge of Top, ss into next dc, ss into each of 6 ch, ss into 4th of 14 ch. Cut yarn and fasten off.

Making up

Place the Top and Base pieces together, right sides out, lining up edges. Join, stitch by stitch, with dc (see page 17), inserting the hook into one loop only on both edges. When seam is two-thirds complete, insert the cushion pad and continue joining the two edges; fasten off and weave in tails of yarn.

On close inspection, you can see the dewdrop effect of the little glass beads on the cobweb. If you cannot find this yarn – or a similar beaded double-knitting yarn – you could add beads to your own choice of yarn. To do this, thread a loop of sewing thread into a fine needle, pass the tail of the ball of yarn through the loop of thread, then thread beads on to the needle, slipping them down over the thread and on to the yarn.

Bobble

A richly textured crochet stitch creates a cushion that is very tactile. Use a luxury yarn spun from wool and cashmere and you have a cushion that you won't be able to keep your hands off.

CUSHION PATTERN

This cushion is worked in a bobble pattern, which creates a rich texture. To make a five-treble bobble, wrap the yarn over the hook and work the first treble, omitting the last stage, to leave two loops on the hook; work the second, third, fourth and fifth trebles in the same way; you now have six loops on the hook. Wrap the yarn around the hook and draw it through the six loops to complete the bobble. Add a chain stitch to secure the top of the bobble. Bobbles are worked on wrong-side rows and are pushed to the front of the work. The back of the cushion is worked in two halves, with a slight overlap, in rows of double crochet.

Tension

15 sts and 20 rows to 10cm (4in), measured over rows of double crochet, using 5.00mm (US H/8, UK 6) hook.

Front

Foundation chain: with 5.00mm (US H/8, UK 6) hook, make 47 ch.

Foundation row: 1 dc in 2nd ch from hook, 1 dc in each ch to end; turn (46 sts).

Row 1 (WS): 1 ch (does not count as a st), 1 dc in 1st 2 dc, (1 dc in next dc, 5-tr bobble in next dc, 1 dc in each of next 2 dc) 11 times; turn.

Row 2: 1 ch, 1 dc in 1st 2 dc, (1 dc in each of 1st 2 dc, 1 dc in top of bobble, 1 dc in each of next 3 dc) 11 times; turn.

Row 3: 1 ch (does not count as a st), 1 dc in each of 1st 5 dc, (5-tr bobble in next dc, 1 dc in each of next 3 dc) 10 times, 1 dc in last dc; turn.

Row 4: 1 ch, 1 dc in 1st dc, (1 dc in each of next 3 dc, 1 dc in top of bobble) 10 times, 1 dc in each of last 5 dc; turn.

Rep rows 1–4 13 times, then rows 1 and 2 once more.
Cut yarn and fasten off.

EQUIPMENT

YARN:
Wool–cashmere blend aran (worsted) yarn, 6 x 50g (1¾oz) balls in mulberry

HOOK:
5.00mm (US H/8, UK 6)

CUSHION PAD:
Rectangular, 40 x 35cm (16 x 14in)

MEASUREMENTS:
40 x 35cm (16 x 14in)

Yarn Notes

This cushion has been made using Debbie Bliss Cashmerino Aran, which is a blend of 55 per cent merino wool, 33 per cent microfibre and 12 per cent cashmere, making it soft and luxurious but also very practical. There are 90m (98½ yds) in a 50g (1¾oz) ball. As this cushion features a thickly textured pattern, it uses a large quantity of yarn compared with cushions of a similar size with a thinner, flatter fabric. Substitute another aran (worsted) yarn, if you like, but be sure to check the tension or your cushion cover may turn out smaller or larger than the one shown here, in which case you will need a different sized cushion pad.

Back (make two)

Foundation chain: with 5.00mm (US H/8, UK 6) hook, make 47 ch.

Foundation row: 1 dc in 2nd ch from hook, 1 dc in each ch to end; turn (46 sts).

Row 1: 1 ch (does not count as a st), 1 dc in each dc of previous row.

Rep row 1 33 times.

Cut yarn and fasten off.

(Do not cut yarn after completing second Back piece.)

Making up

With right sides out, line up the foundation edge of one of the Back pieces with the foundation edge of the Front and pin together. Line up the last row of the second piece with the last row of the Front and pin together. Pin sides, overlapping the two remaining edges of the Back pieces. Join Back to Front all round with a double crochet seam (see page 17).

The pattern of raised bobbles not only looks attractive but it feels lovely to the touch – but bear in mind that a richly textured crochet stitch pattern like this uses a lot more yarn than a flat fabric does.

Use a double crochet seam to join the Back and Front pieces together: this forms a really neat, discreet edge.

Bobbles are worked on every wrong-side row, and are offset, so they form a kind of trellis pattern of neat diagonal lines.

Zigzag

Choose two subtle colours for this cushion, for an understated effect that will suit most modern interiors – and even a few traditional ones, too. A soft yarn produces a comfy cushion than will soften a hard chair and can be used in almost any room in the house.

CUSHION PATTERN

This cushion is worked in a wavy zigzag stitch. It is worked in one piece, with buttonholes worked into the last row.

Tension

Measured over pattern using 4.00mm (US G/6, UK 8) hook and recommended yarn, one pattern repeat measures 7cm (2¾in) and one zigzag stripe is 25mm (1in) wide.

Front and Back

Foundation chain: using 4.00mm (US G/6, UK 8) hook and yarn A, make 72 ch.

Foundation row: 1 tr in 3rd ch from hook, 2 tr in same place, *1 tr in each of next 3 ch, (tr3tog over next 3 ch) twice, 1 tr in each of next 3 ch, (3 tr in next ch) twice; rep from * to end, finishing with 3 tr in last ch; turn.

Row 1: 3 ch (counts as 1 tr), 2 tr in 1st st, *1 tr in each of next 3 sts, (tr3tog over next 3 sts) twice, 1 tr in each of next 3 sts, (3 tr in next st) twice; rep from * to end, ending with 3 tr in top of turning ch and joining in yarn B in last part of 3rd tr; turn.

Rows 2 and 3: as row 1, using yarn B; change to yarn A in last part of 3rd tr; turn.

Rows 4 and 5: as row 1 using yarn A; change to yarn B in last part of 3rd tr; turn.

Rep rows 2–5 16 times, then rows 2–4 once more.

Next row (buttonholes): 3 ch (counts as 1 tr), 2 tr in 1st st, *1 tr in each of next 3 sts, (tr3tog over next 3 sts) twice, 1 tr in each of next 3 sts, 1 tr in next st, 4 ch, 1 tr in next st); rep from * four times more; 1 tr in each of next 3 sts, (tr3tog over next 3 sts) twice, 1 tr in each of next 3 sts, 3 tr in turning ch.

Cut yarn and fasten off.

EQUIPMENT

YARN:
Cotton and kapok blend DK (8-ply) yarn, 2 x 100g (3½oz) balls each in cream (A) and beige (B)

HOOK:
4.00mm (US G/6, UK 8)

CUSHION PAD:
Rectangular, 45 x 35cm (18 x 14in)

OTHER ITEMS:
4 round buttons, 2cm (¾in) in diameter

MEASUREMENTS:
45 x 35cm (18 x 14in)

Yarn Notes

This cushion has been made using Sublime Baby Cotton Kapok DK, a natural blend of 85 per cent cotton and 15 per cent kapok that produces a fabric that is firm but soft to the touch. There are 116m (127 yds) in a 50g (1¾oz) ball. A yarn like this, made from natural fibres, is cool in the summer and warm in the winter. This is a standard DK (8-ply) weight, so if you cannot find this yarn, it should be easy to substitute another.

Making up

Place the cover right side up on the work surface and fold the end with the buttonholes over by 13cm (5in) and the other end over by 41cm (16in), so that it overlaps. Check that the overall length of the cover is now 45cm (18in); adjust if necessary. Pin the sides together, then stitch the seam in backstitch (see page 14). Turn right sides out.

Stitch the buttons in place, to correspond with the buttonholes.

The first and last few rows overlap at one end of the cushion cover and the gap is fastened neatly with four buttons that align with the four zigzag points on the last row of the pattern.

Button loops are created on the last row by replacing four of the trebles that from the upper point – the 'peak' – of the zigzag with four chain stitches.

Choose buttons that match one of the yarn colours for an elegant, classy look or, if you prefer, you could make more of a feature of the buttons by choosing a contrasting colour.

Chair Square

This flat cushion is designed as a seat cushion for a kitchen or dining room chair. Use a piece of foam or thick wadding cut to size, to soften a hard seat and make dining much more comfortable – and stylish.

CUSHION PATTERN

This cushion is worked in rounds of double crochet, with the hook inserted into the back loop only of each stitch throughout.

Tension

18 sts and 24 rows to 10cm (4in), measured over rows of dc using 3.50mm hook (US E/4, UK 9).

Side 1

Foundation round: with 3.50mm (US E/4, UK 9) hook and yarn A, make a magic ring and work 1 ch, 12 dc in ring; join with a ss to 1st dc of round (12 sts).

Round 1: 1 ch (does not count as a stitch), 1 dc in each of 1st 2 dc, 3 dc in next dc, (1 dc in each of next 2 dc, 3 dc in next dc) three times; join with a ss to 1st dc of round (20 sts).

Round 2: 1 ch, 1 dc in each of 1st 3 dc, 3 dc in next dc, (1 dc in each of next 4 dc, 3 dc in next dc) three times, 1 dc in last dc; join with a ss to 1st dc of round (28 sts).

Round 3: 1 ch, 1 dc in each of 1st 4 dc, 3 dc in next dc, (1 dc in each of next 6 dc, 3 dc in next dc) three times, 1 dc in each of last 2 dc; join with a ss to 1st dc of round (36 sts).

Round 4: 1 ch, 1 dc in each of 1st 5 dc, 3 dc in next dc, (1 dc in each of next 8 dc, 3 dc in next dc) three times, 1 dc in each of last 3 dc; join with a ss to 1st dc of round (44 sts).

Round 5: 1 ch, 1 dc in each of 1st 6 dc, 3 dc in next dc, (1 dc in each of next 10 dc, 3 dc in next dc) three times, 1 dc in each of last 4 dc; join with a ss to 1st dc of round (52 sts).

Round 6: 1 ch, 1 dc in each of 1st 7 dc, 3 dc in next dc, (1 dc in each of next 12 dc, 3 dc in next dc) three times, 1 dc in each of last 5 dc; join with a ss to 1st dc of round (60 sts).

Round 7: 1 ch, 1 dc in each of 1st 8 dc, 3 dc in next dc, (1 dc in each of next 14 dc, 3 dc in next dc) three times, 1 dc in each of last 6 dc; join with a ss to 1st dc of round (68 sts).

Round 8: 1 ch, 1 dc in each of 1st 9 dc, 3 dc in next dc, (1 dc in each of next 16 dc, 3 dc in next dc) three times, 1 dc in each of last 7 dc; join with a ss to 1st dc of round (76 sts).

Round 9: 1 ch, 1 dc in each of 1st 10 dc, 3 dc in next dc, (1 dc in each of next 18 dc, 3 dc in next dc) three times, 1 dc in each of last 8 dc; join with a ss to 1st dc of round (84 sts).

EQUIPMENT

YARN:
Bamboo-wool blend DK (8-ply) yarn, 2 x 50g (1¾oz) balls in china blue (A) and 1 x 50g ball each in pale blue (B), kiwi (C) and ivory (D)

HOOK:
3.50mm (US E/4, UK 9)

CUSHION PAD:
Square of foam or polyester wadding, 35 x 35cm (14 x 14in), 2.5cm (1in) thick

MEASUREMENTS:
36 x 36cm (14½ x 14½in) square, including border

Yarn Notes

This cushion has been made using Sirdar Snuggly Baby Bamboo, which is a blend of 80 per cent bamboo-sourced viscose and 20 per cent wool, creating a soft fabric with a slight stretch. There are 95m (104 yds) in a 50g (1¾oz) ball.

Round 10: 1 ch, 1 dc in each of 1st 11 dc, 3 dc in next dc, (1 dc in each of next 20 dc, 3 dc in next dc) three times, 1 dc in each of last 9 dc; join with a ss to 1st dc of round (92 sts).

Round 11: 1 ch, 1 dc in each of 1st 12 dc, 3 dc in next dc, (1 dc in each of next 22 dc, 3 dc in next dc) three times, 1 dc in each of last 10 dc; join with a ss to 1st dc of round (100 sts).

Round 12: 1 ch, 1 dc in each of 1st 13 dc, 3 dc in next dc, (1 dc in each of next 24 dc, 3 dc in next dc) three times, 1 dc in each of last 11 dc; join with a ss to 1st dc of round (108 sts).

Round 13: 1 ch, 1 dc in each of 1st 14 dc, 3 dc in next dc, (1 dc in each of next 26 dc, 3 dc in next dc) three times, 1 dc in each of last 12 dc; join with a ss to 1st dc of round (116 sts).

Round 14: 1 ch, 1 dc in each of 1st 15 dc, 3 dc in next dc, (1 dc in each of next 28 dc, 3 dc in next dc) three times, 1 dc in each of last 13 dc; join with a ss to 1st dc of round (124 sts).

Round 15: 1 ch, 1 dc in each of 1st 16 dc, 3 dc in next dc, (1 dc in each of next 30 dc, 3 dc in next dc) three times, 1 dc in each of last 14 dc; join with a ss to 1st dc of round (132 sts).

Round 16: 1 ch, 1 dc in each of 1st 17 dc, 3 dc in next dc, (1 dc in each of next 32 dc, 3 dc in next dc) three times, 1 dc in each of last 15 dc; join with a ss to 1st dc of round (140 sts).

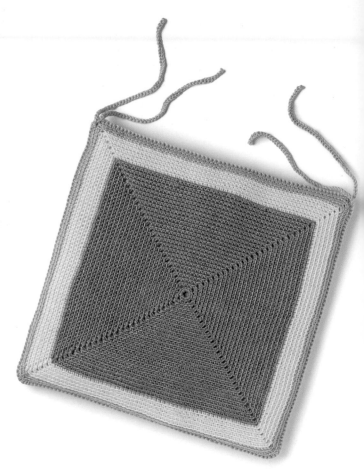

Round 17: 1 ch, 1 dc in each of 1st 18 dc, 3 dc in next dc, (1 dc in each of next 34 dc, 3 dc in next dc) three times, 1 dc in each of last 16 dc; join with a ss to 1st dc of round (148 sts).

Round 18: 1 ch, 1 dc in each of 1st 19 dc, 3 dc in next dc, (1 dc in each of next 36 dc, 3 dc in next dc) three times, 1 dc in each of last 17 dc; join with a ss to 1st dc of round (156 sts).

Round 19: 1 ch, 1 dc in each of 1st 20 dc, 3 dc in next dc, (1 dc in each of next 38 dc, 3 dc in next dc) three times, 1 dc in each of last 18 dc; join with a ss to 1st dc of round (164 sts).

Round 20: 1 ch, 1 dc in each of 1st 21 dc, 3 dc in next dc, (1 dc in each of next 40 dc, 3 dc in next dc) three times, 1 dc in each of last 19 dc; join with a ss to 1st dc of round (172 sts).

Round 21: 1 ch, 1 dc in each of 1st 22 dc, 3 dc in next dc, (1 dc in each of next 42 dc, 3 dc in next dc) three times, 1 dc in each of last 20 dc; join with a ss to 1st dc of round (180 sts); cut A and join in B.

Round 22: 1 ch, 1 dc in each of 1st 23 dc, 3 dc in next dc, (1 dc in each of next 44 dc, 3 dc in next dc) three times, 1 dc in each of last 21 dc; join with a ss to 1st dc of round (188 sts).

Round 23: 1 ch, 1 dc in each of 1st 24 dc, 3 dc in next dc, (1 dc in each of next 46 dc, 3 dc in next dc) three times, 1 dc in each of last 22 dc; join with a ss to 1st dc of round (196 sts).

Round 24: 1 ch, 1 dc in each of 1st 25 dc, 3 dc in next dc, (1 dc in each of next 48 dc, 3 dc in next dc) three times, 1 dc in each of last 23 dc; join with a ss to 1st dc of round (204 sts).

Round 25: 1 ch, 1 dc in each of 1st 26 dc, 3 dc in next dc, (1 dc in each of next 50 dc, 3 dc in next dc) three times, 1 dc in each of last 24 dc; join with a ss to 1st dc of round (212 sts).

Round 26: 1 ch, 1 dc in each of 1st 27 dc, 3 dc in next dc, (1 dc in each of next 52 dc, 3 dc in next dc) three times, 1 dc in each of last 25 dc; join with a ss to 1st dc of round (220 sts).

Round 27: 1 ch, 1 dc in each of 1st 28 dc, 3 dc in next dc, (1 dc in each of next 54 dc, 3 dc in next dc) three times, 1 dc in each of last 26 dc; join with a ss to 1st dc of round (228 sts).

Round 28: 1 ch, 1 dc in each of 1st 29 dc, 3 dc in next dc, (1 dc in each of next 56 dc, 3 dc in next dc) three times, 1 dc in each of last 27 dc; join with a ss to 1st dc of round (236 sts).

Round 29: 1 ch, 1 dc in each of 1st 30 dc, 3 dc in next dc, (1 dc in each of next 58 dc, 3 dc in next dc) three times, 1 dc in each of last 28 dc; join with a ss to 1st dc of round (244 sts).

Round 30: 1 ch, 1 dc in each of 1st 31 dc, 3 dc in next dc, (1 dc in each of next 60 dc, 3 dc in next dc) three times, 1 dc in each of last 29 dc; join with a ss to 1st dc of round (252 sts); cut B and join in C.

Round 31: 1 ch, 1 dc in each of 1st 32 dc, 3 dc in next dc, (1 dc in each of next 62 dc, 3 dc in next dc) three times, 1 dc in each of last 30 dc; join with a ss to 1st dc of round (260 sts).

Cut yarn and fasten off.

Side 2

Follow instructions for Side 1 but use yarn D instead of yarn B. After completing Round 32, do not cut yarn C.

Making up

Place two pieces together, right sides out, lining up edges and corners.

Border and ties

1 ch, 1 dc in each of 1st 33 dc, 1 dc in corner, (46 ch, 1 ss in 2nd ch from hook, 1 ss in each of next 44 ch, 1 ss in corner st) twice, 1 dc in each of next 64 dc, (46 ch, 1 ss in 2nd ch from hook, 1 ss in each of next 44 ch, 1 ss in corner st) twice (1 dc in each of next 64 dc, 3 dc in next dc) twice, inserting cushion pad after 1st repeat, 1 dc in each of last 31 dc; join with a ss to 1st dc of round.

Cut yarn and fasten off.

Weave in all remaining ends.

Worked in the round, the square shape is formed by working extra stitches into each of the four corners on every round.

Mix and match colours to suit your own tastes. The central square and border both require approximately one 50g (1¾oz) ball of the recommended yarn – but you can add a few rows in another colour, if necessary, if you run out.

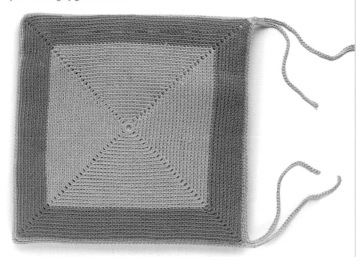

Carnival

Sometimes we all need a big splash of cheerful colour in our lives. As a bonus, this pair of square cushions, crocheted in single-row stripes, will use up any odds and ends of yarn from your work basket, so that should put a smile on your face! Instructions for the larger cushion are given in square brackets throughout.

CUSHION PATTERN

Each of these cushions is worked in rows of half treble crochet, changing colour after every row. You can choose to weave in some of the yarn tails as you go, or leave them until the making-up stage and use them for stitching the seams. These cushions are a great way of using up small scraps: as a guide, one row of the larger cushion requires approximately 3m (10ft) of yarn, while one row of the smaller cushion requires about 2.6m (8½ft).

Tension

15 sts and 13 rows to 10cm (4in), measured over rows of htr using 4.00mm (US G/6, UK 8) hook.

Side 1

Foundation chain: using 4.00mm (US G/6, UK 8) hook and first colour, make 40 [50]ch.

Foundation row: 1 htr in 3rd ch from hook, 1 htr in each ch to end; join in new colour in last stage of last htr and cut old colour, leaving a tail; turn (38 [48] sts).

Row 1: 2 ch (counts as 1 htr), 1 htr in each htr of previous row, 1 htr in top of 2 turning ch; join in new colour in last stage of last htr and cut old colour, leaving a tail; turn.

Row 2: 2 ch, 1 htr in each htr of previous row, 1 htr in top of 2 ch; join in new colour in last stage of last htr and cut old colour, leaving a tail; turn.

Rep row 2 32 [40] times, changing colour at the end of every row.

Fasten off.

Side 2

Follow instructions for Side 1, using a different assortment of colours.

EQUIPMENT

YARN:

Acrylic DK (8-ply) yarn in a range of colours, approximately 200m (219 yds), 90g (3¼oz) for small cushion [300m (328 yds), 110g (4oz) for large cushion]

HOOK:

4.00mm (US G/6, UK 8)

CUSHION PADS:

Square, 25 x 25cm (10 x 10in) [35 x 35cm (14 x 14in)]

OTHER ITEMS:

Bobble braid, 105cm (41in) [150cm (59in)] long
Sewing needle
Sewing thread to match braid

MEASUREMENTS:

25 x 25cm (10 x 10in) [35 x 35cm (14 x 14in)]

Yarn Notes

Acrylic yarns are cheap to manufacture, hard-wearing and resistant to moths. They are widely available, particularly in DK (8-ply) weight, and have been chosen here for their bright, almost luminous colours. Many manufacturers package colourful acrylic yarns in 25g (1oz) balls, and sometimes in value packs containing a number of balls of different colours, to allow you to mix and match colours without spending too much money.

Making up

Place the two pieces together, right sides together, lining up the edges. Join the two foundation rows stitch by stitch, by oversewing or using the flat seam method (see pages 15 and 16). Turn wrong sides out and stitch side seams in backstitch (see page 14). Turn right sides out, insert the cushion pad and join the two last rows stitch by stitch, by oversewing or using the flat seam method. Pin the bobble braid over the seams on all four sides, then oversew both edges in place using a sewing needle and thread to match the braid (see top tip box, right).

TOP TIP

TOP TIP

Before stitching, you may find it helpful to pin the braid in place all around the cushion, making sure that the flat part of the braid covers the seams, for a neat finish, and that none of the bobbles is trapped. Thread a sewing needle with thread to match the braid and slipstitch the edges of the braid to the cushion cover.

Bobble braid is brilliant for adding an eye-catching border to a cushion quickly and easily, and it is easily available, in a good range of colours.

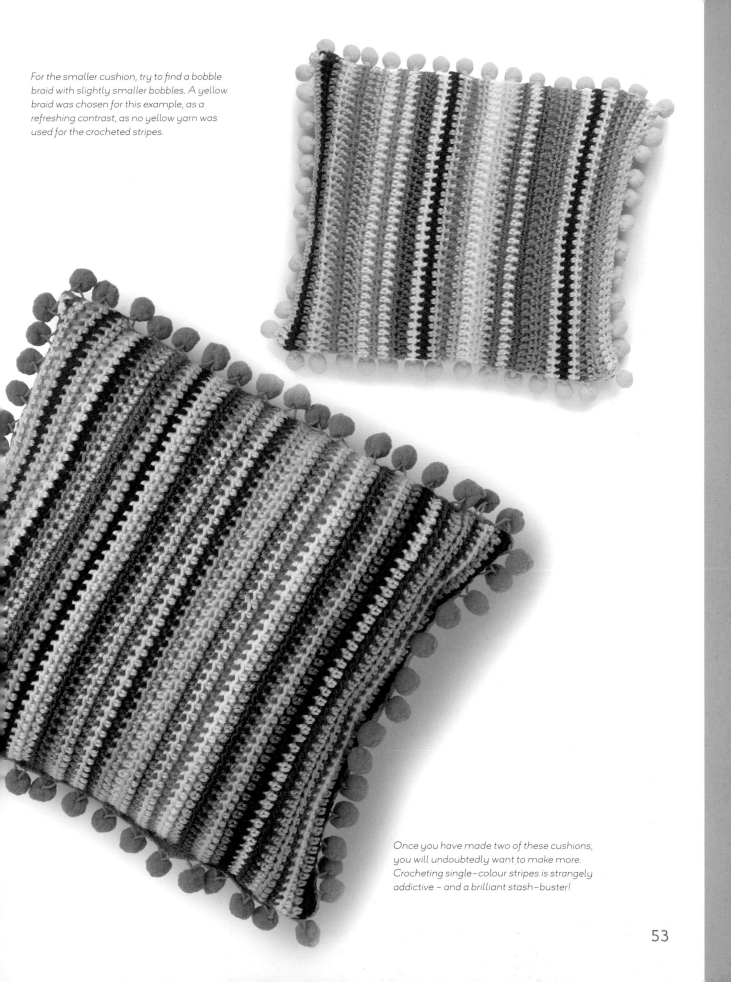

For the smaller cushion, try to find a bobble braid with slightly smaller bobbles. A yellow braid was chosen for this example, as a refreshing contrast, as no yellow yarn was used for the crocheted stripes.

Once you have made two of these cushions, you will undoubtedly want to make more. Crocheting single-colour stripes is strangely addictive – and a brilliant stash-buster!

Granny

The granny square is a universal favourite and one of the first patterns many people learn to crochet. Constructed from 32 squares, in a comfy yarn made from a blend of wool and cotton, this generous-sized cushion showcases the granny square and is a real classic.

CUSHION PATTERN

This cushion is made up from 32 granny squares. This pattern is for a classic granny square, which differs slightly from the version on pages 86–89. Each round is worked in a different colour, creating lots of yarn ends: you can leave these until the making-up stage and darn them all in, or you can work over most of them as you go along, if you find this easier.

Tension

One square measures approximately 11cm (4½in) using 4.50mm (US 7, UK 7) hook and the recommended yarn.

Granny square (make 32)

Foundation chain: with 4.50mm (US 7, UK 7) hook and your choice of yarn A, B, C, D or E, make 4 ch, join with ss to 1st ch to make a ring.

Round 1: 3 ch (counts as 1 tr), 2 tr into ring, 3 ch, (3 tr in ring, 3 ch) three times, join with ss to 3rd of 3 ch; cut yarn and join a second colour to any 3-ch sp.

Round 2: 3 ch, 2 tr in 3-ch sp, 3 ch, 3 tr in same sp, 1 ch, *(3 tr, 3 ch, 3 tr) in next 3-ch sp, 1 ch, rep from * twice more, join with ss to 3rd of 3 ch; cut yarn and join a third colour to any 3-ch corner sp.

Round 3: 3 ch, 2 tr in 3-ch sp, 3 ch, 3 tr in same sp, 1 ch, 3 tr in 1-ch sp, 1 ch, *(3 tr, 3 ch, 3 tr) in next 3-ch sp, 1 ch, 3 tr in next 1-ch sp, 1 ch, rep from * twice more, join with ss to 3rd of 3 ch; cut yarn and join yarn F to any 3-ch corner sp.

Round 4: 4 ch (counts as 1 tr, 1 ch), *(3 tr in next 1-ch sp, 1 ch), twice, (3 tr, 3 ch, 3 tr) in next corner sp, 1 ch, rep from * twice more, (3 tr in next 1-ch space, 1 ch) twice, (3 tr, 3 ch, 2 tr) in corner sp; join with ss to 3rd of 4 ch.

EQUIPMENT

YARN:

Wool-cotton blend DK (8-ply) yarn, 1 x 50g (1¾oz) ball each in pale blue (A), pale lime (B), orange (C), damson (D) and green (E) and 2 x 50g (1¾oz) balls in deep coral (F)

HOOK:

4.50mm (US 7, UK 7)

CUSHION PAD:

Square, 45 x 45cm (18 x 18in), covered in orange or other brightly coloured fabric

MEASUREMENTS:

45 x 45cm (18 x 18in), including border

Yarn Notes

This cushion has been made using Amy Butler Belle Organic DK from Rowan, a yarn with a fairly loose twist, a 50:50 blend of organic wool and organic cotton. The resulting fabric is nice and soft. There are 120m (131 yds) in a 50g (1¾oz) ball. You could substitute another DK (8-ply) weight yarn but you may have to allow a little more yarn to complete the cushion.

Making up

Join 16 squares to make the Front and the same for the Back. Use the flat seam technique for the neatest result (see page 16).

You can either stitch Back and Front together or work a border, as follows:

Round 1: place Back and Front together, right sides out, lining up edges. Join yarn F to one corner space, inserting it through both corresponding spaces and work 3 dc in corner sp, then work *(1 dc in each of next 3 tr, inserting hook through sts on both Back and Front covers, 1 dc in next sp) four times, 2 dc in end of seam; rep from * to next corner and work 5 dc in corner sp.

Do the same around next two sides, insert the cushion pad and work along rem side, finishing with 2 dc in first corner sp; join with a ss to 1st dc of round.

Round 2: 1 ch, 1 dc in each dc of previous round, except 3 dc in each corner st; join with a ss to 1st dc of round.

Cut yarn and fasten off. To create pompoms, see right.

CREATING POMPOMS

This big, bright cushion looks even better with a decorative pompom on each corner. Cut a piece of sturdy card measuring approximately 13 x 8cm (5 x 3in) and wind spare yarn around the card to form a thick bundle. Slip a length of yarn under the bundle, tie in a tight knot, then cut through all the loops of yarn on either side. Fluff out with your fingers, then trim the ends with scissors to create a neat, round pompom.

For a quirky finish, make each of the pompoms in a different colour, picking out colours that have been used in the granny squares.

Big, soft pompoms add texture, detail and a sense of fun. Make sure you stitch them securely to the corners of the cushion cover.

You will be able to see the cushion pad through the holes in the crocheted fabric, so cover the pad in a plain coloured fabric to match or complement the main yarn colour.

Waves

This gorgeous cushion is made up of rows of shells that are interspersed with rows of double crochet, using contrasting colours to emphasise the wavy pattern. This cushion is perfect for all kinds of places, including the garden or patio – or even the beach.

CUSHION PATTERN

This cushion is worked in a wavy shell stitch. It is worked in one piece, with buttonholes worked into the last two rows. The button covers are worked in the round.

Tension

21 sts and 12 rows, measured over pattern using 4.00mm (US G/6, UK 8) hook and recommended yarn.

Front and Back

Foundation chain: using 4.00mm (US G/6, UK 8) hook and yarn A, make 58 ch.

Foundation row: 1 dc in 2nd ch from hook, 1 dc in each ch to end (57 sts).

Row 1 (RS): 3 ch (counts as 1 tr), 3 tr into 1st dc, *miss 3 dc, 1 dc in each of next 7 dc, miss 3 dc, 7 tr in next dc; rep from * to last st, 4 tr in last dc; turn.

Row 2: 1 ch (does not count as a st), 1 dc in each st to end, working last dc in top of 3 ch; turn.

Row 3: 1 ch, 1 dc in each of 1st 4 dc, *miss 3 dc, 7 tr in next dc, miss 3 dc, 1 dc in each 1 dc in each of next 7 dc; rep from * to last 11 sts, miss 3 dc, 7 tr in next dc, miss 3 dc, 1 dc in each of last 4 dc; turn.

Row 4: 1 ch, 1 dc in each st of previous row; turn.

Row 5: 3 ch (counts as 1 tr), 3 tr into 1st dc, *miss 3 dc, 1 dc in each of next 7 dc, miss 3 dc, 7 tr in next dc; rep from * to last st, 4 tr in last dc; turn; do not cut A but join in B.

Row 6: using B, 1 ch, 1 dc in each st to end, working last dc in top of 3 ch; turn; cut B and continue in A.

Row 7: 1 ch, 1 dc in each of 1st 4 dc, *miss 3 dc, 7 tr in next dc, miss 3 dc, 1 dc in each 1 dc in each of next 7 dc; rep from * to last 11 sts, miss 3 dc, 7 tr in next dc, miss 3 dc, 1 dc in each of last 4 dc; turn.

Row 8: 1 ch, 1 dc in each st of previous row; turn.

Row 9: 3 ch (counts as 1 tr), 3 tr into 1st dc, *miss 3 dc, 1 dc in each of next 7 dc, miss 3 dc, 7 tr in next dc; rep from * to last st, 4 tr in last dc; turn; do not cut A but join in C.

Row 10: using C, 1 ch, 1 dc in each st to end, working last dc in top of 3 ch; turn; cut C and continue in A.

EQUIPMENT

YARN:
100 per cent cotton DK (8-ply) yarn, 2 x 100g (3½oz) balls in jade green (A) and 1 x 100g ball each in purple (B) and navy (C)

HOOK:
4.00mm (US G/6, UK 8)

CUSHION PAD:
Rectangular, 40 x 30cm (16 x 12in)

OTHER ITEMS:
3 round buttons, 25mm (1in) diameter

MEASUREMENTS:
40 x 30cm (16 x 12in)

Yarn Notes

This cushion has been made using Patons 100 per cent Cotton DK, a tightly spun mercerised cotton available in a good range of colours. There are 330m (360 yds) in a 100g (3½oz) ball. A classic cotton yarn like this is the perfect choice for fancy crochet stitches, as it provides excellent stitch definition.

Row 11: 1 ch, 1 dc in each of 1st 4 dc, *miss 3 dc, 7 tr in next dc, miss 3 dc, 1 dc in each 1 dc in each of next 7 dc; rep from * to last 11 sts, miss 3 dc, 7 tr in next dc, miss 3 dc, 1 dc in each of last 4 dc; turn.

Row 12: 1 ch, 1 dc in each st of previous row; turn.

Row 13: 3 ch (counts as 1 tr), 3 tr into 1st dc, *miss 3 dc, 1 dc in each of next 7 dc, miss 3 dc, 7 tr in next dc; rep from * to last st, 4 tr in last dc; turn; do not cut A but join in B.

Rep rows 6–13 13 times, then rows 6–8 once.

Next row (buttonholes): 3 ch (counts as 1 tr), 3 tr into 1st dc, *miss 3 dc, 1 dc in each of next 7 dc, miss 3 dc, 1 tr, 5 ch, 1 tr in next dc; rep from * to last st, 4 tr in last dc; turn; cut A and join in C.

Next row: 1 ch, 1 dc in each of 1st 12 sts, 5 dc into 5-ch sp, (1 dc into each of next 9 sts, 5 dc into 5-ch sp) twice, 1 dc in each st to end.

Cut yarn and fasten off.

Button covers (make three)

Foundation round: using 4.00mm (US G/6, UK 8) hook and yarn A, make a magic ring and work 1 ch (does not count as a st), 8 dc in ring; join with a ss to 1st dc (8 sts).

Round 1: 1 ch, 2 dc in each dc of previous round; join with a ss to 1st dc (16 sts).

Round 2: 1 ch, 1 dc in 1st dc, (2 dc in next dc, 1 dc in next dc) seven times, 2 dc in last dc; join with a ss to 1st dc (24 sts).

Round 3: 1 ch, then inserting hook into back loop only of each st, (dc2tog) 12 times (12 sts).

Cut yarn, leaving a tail, and fasten off.

Making up

Place the cover right side up on the work surface and fold the end with the buttonholes over by 13cm (5in) and the other end over by 33cm (13in), so that it overlaps. Check that the overall length of the cover is now 40cm (16in); adjust if necessary. Pin the sides together, then stitch the seam in backstitch (see page 14). Turn right sides out.

For the covered buttons, thread the tail of yarn into a tapestry needle and pass the needle in and out of the stitch loops all around the edge of the Button Cover. Place a button inside and pull up the yarn tail to enclose the button; fasten off the yarn tail firmly, then use it to stitch the button in place, to correspond with one of the buttonholes. Repeat for the other two buttons.

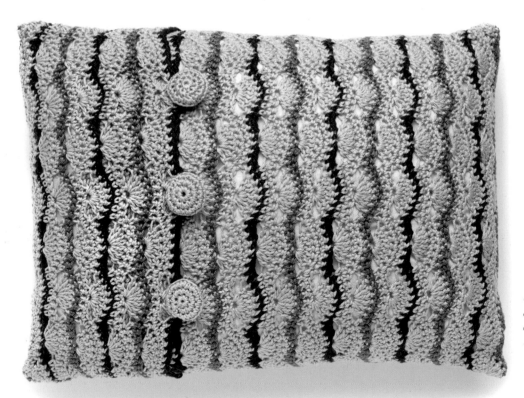

Using contrasting colours emphasises the wave pattern and draws attention to the intricacy of your stitches.

Covered buttons are easy to make and add a really professional finish. You can use any buttons – ones with holes or shanks – as long as they are the right size to fit the cover.

The shell pattern is formed by making groups of seven trebles. Shell rows are alternated with rows of double crochet, some of which are worked in contrast colours.

Caravan

A bolster cushion is a very useful shape, placed across one end of a couch, or behind other cushions for added support. This brightly striped bolster cover would not look out of place in a caravan or beach hut, or anywhere you wish to add a splash of colour as well as a bit of comfort.

CUSHION PATTERN

The circular ends of this cushion are worked in rounds of double crochet. You will need to work increases on every other round to create the circular shape. The main part of the cushion is worked separately, in one tubular piece. The two end pieces are joined to either end of the tube with double crochet seams.

Tension

18 sts and 20 rows to 10cm (4in), measured over rows of dc using 3.75mm (US F/5, UK 8 or 9) hook.

Ends (make two)

Foundation round: with 3.75mm (US F/5, UK 8 or 9) hook, make a magic ring and work 1 ch, 6 dc in ring; join with a ss to 1st dc of round (6 sts).

Round 1: 1 ch (does not count as a stitch), 2 dc in each dc of previous round; join with a ss to 1st dc of round (12 sts).

Round 2: 1 ch, 2 dc in each dc of previous round; join with a ss to 1st dc of round (24 sts).

Round 3: 1 ch, 1 dc in each dc of previous round; join with a ss to 1st dc of round.

Round 4: 1 ch, 1 dc in 1st dc, 2 dc in next dc, (1 dc in next dc, 2 dc in next dc) 11 times; join with a ss to 1st dc of round (36 sts).

Round 5: 1 ch, 1 dc in each dc of previous round; join with a ss to 1st dc of round.

Round 6: 1 ch, 1 dc in 1st dc, 1 dc in next dc, 2 dc in next dc, (1 dc in each of next 2 dc, 2 dc in next dc) 11 times; join with a ss to 1st dc of round (48 sts).

Round 7: 1 ch, 1 dc in each dc of previous round; join with a ss to 1st dc of round.

Round 8: 1 ch, 1 dc in 1st dc, 1 dc in each of next 2 dc, 2 dc in next dc, (1 dc in each of next 3 dc, 2 dc in next dc) 11 times; join with a ss to 1st dc of round (60 sts).

Round 9: 1 ch, 1 dc in each dc of previous round; join with a ss to 1st dc of round.

Round 10: 1 ch, 1 dc in 1st dc, 1 dc in each of next 3 dc, 2 dc in next dc, (1 dc in each of next 4 dc, 2 dc in next dc) 11 times; join with a ss to 1st dc of round (72 sts).

Round 11: 1 ch, 1 dc in each dc of previous round; join with a ss to 1st dc of round.

EQUIPMENT

YARN:
Custom-made multicoloured DK (8-ply) yarn (see Yarn Notes below), approximately 480m (525 yds), 375g (13¼oz)

HOOK:
3.75mm (US F/5, UK 8 or 9)

CUSHION PAD:
Bolster, 48cm (19in) long, 18cm (7in) diameter

MEASUREMENTS
48cm (19in) long, 18cm (7in) diameter

Yarn Notes

Acrylic yarns are cheap and widely available in a dazzling choice of colours. If you are cost-conscious and keen to make use of even the tiniest little scrap left over from your crochet and knitting projects, you can combine them to create a unique multi-coloured yarn. Knot the ends of short lengths of acrylic DK (8-ply) yarn together, leaving ends of about 1.5cm (½in), then wind into a ball, ready for use. As you use your composite yarn, each time you encounter a knot, push it through to the wrong side of the work and work stitches over the yarn ends to hide them.

Round 12: 1 ch, 1 dc in 1st dc, 1 dc in each of next 4 dc, 2 dc in next dc, (1 dc in each of next 5 dc, 2 dc in next dc) 11 times; join with a ss to 1st dc of round (84 sts).

Round 13: 1 ch, 1 dc in each dc of previous round; join with a ss to 1st dc of round.

Round 14: 1 ch, 1 dc in 1st dc, 1 dc in each of next 5 dc, 2 dc in next dc, (1 dc in each of next 6 dc, 2 dc in next dc) 11 times; join with a ss to 1st dc of round (96 sts).

Round 15: 1 ch, 1 dc in each dc of previous round; join with a ss to 1st dc of round.

Cut yarn and fasten off.

Tube

Foundation chain: with 3.75mm (US F/5, UK 8 or 9) hook, make 96 ch and join with a ss to 1st ch to make a ring.

Foundation round: 1 ch (does not count as a st), 1 dc in each ch; join with a ss to 1st dc (96 sts).

Round 1: 1 ch, 1 dc in each dc of previous round; join with a ss to 1st dc.

Rep round 1 93 times.

Fasten off but do not cut yarn.

Note:

Instead of joining stitches at the end of each round, you can just carry on working in a spiral, working 1 dc into each dc, until the work measures 48cm (19in).

Making up

Place one of the end pieces across the end of the tube (pin in place, if this helps). Join the two edges, stitch by stitch, with double crochet (see page 17), inserting the hook into one loop only on both edges. When you reach the beginning, join with a ss to 1st dc of round. Insert the bolster pad and attach the other end piece in the same way, with a double-crochet seam.

This bolster shape is useful for the end of a sofa or a chaise longue, or across the end of a single bed.

The round end pieces are made separately, then joined to the end of the tube of crochet that covers the body of the cushion pad; the double crochet seam forms an attractive ridge.

When joining pieces of yarn, mix and match as many different colours as you can for a really dazzling effect. When crocheting the cover, as you come to a knot, try to push it to the wrong side of the work.

Disc

In black and white with a touch of red, this disc-shaped cushion is reminiscent of the style of the 1960s. Firm and round, it makes a good seat cushion for a chair, or maybe a bar stool, and will help to soften a hard surface.

CUSHION PATTERN

This cushion is worked in rounds of double crochet. You will need to work increases on every other round to create the circular shape.

Tension

25 sts and 23 rows to 10cm (4in), measured over rows of double crochet, using 3.50mm (US E/4, UK 9) hook.

Side 1

Foundation round: with 3.50mm (US E/4, UK 9) hook and yarn A, make a magic ring and work 1 ch, 6 dc in ring; join with a ss to 1st dc of round (6 sts).

Round 1: 1 ch (does not count as a stitch), 2 dc in each dc of previous round; join with a ss to 1st dc of round (12 sts).

Round 2: 1 ch, 2 dc in each dc of previous round; join with a ss to 1st dc of round (24 sts).

Round 3: 1 ch, 1 dc in each dc of previous round; join with a ss to 1st dc of round.

Round 4: 1 ch, 1 dc in 1st dc, 2 dc in next dc, (1 dc in next dc, 2 dc in next dc) 11 times; join with a ss to 1st dc of round (36 sts).

Round 5: 1 ch, 1 dc in each dc of previous round; join with a ss to 1st dc of round.

Round 6: 1 ch, 1 dc in 1st dc, 1 dc in next dc, 2 dc in next dc, (1 dc in each of next 2 dc, 2 dc in next dc) 11 times; join with a ss to 1st dc of round (48 sts).

Round 7: 1 ch, 1 dc in each dc of previous round; join with a ss to 1st dc of round.

Round 8: 1 ch, 1 dc in 1st dc, 1 dc in each of next 2 dc, 2 dc in next dc, (1 dc in each of next 3 dc, 2 dc in next dc) 11 times; join with a ss to 1st dc of round (60 sts).

Round 9: 1 ch, 1 dc in each dc of previous round; join with a ss to 1st dc of round.

Round 10: 1 ch, 1 dc in 1st dc, 1 dc in each of next 3 dc, 2 dc in next dc, (1 dc in each of next 4 dc, 2 dc in next dc) 11 times; join with a ss to 1st dc of round (72 sts).

Round 11: 1 ch, 1 dc in each dc of previous round; join with a ss to 1st dc of round.

Round 12: 1 ch, 1 dc in 1st dc, 1 dc in each of next 4 dc, 2 dc in next dc, (1 dc in each of next 5 dc, 2 dc in next dc) 11 times; join with a ss to 1st dc of round (84 sts).

Round 13: 1 ch, 1 dc in each dc of previous round; join with a ss to 1st dc of round.

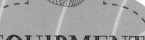

EQUIPMENT

YARN:
Wool-cashmere blend light DK (8-ply) yarn, 2 x 50g (1¾oz) balls each in white (A) and black (C); 1 x 50g (1¾oz) ball in red (B)

HOOK:
3.50mm (US E/4, UK 9)

CUSHION PAD:
Round, 36cm (14½in) diameter

OTHER ITEMS:
Tapestry needle
2 plain buttons with shanks, 4.5cm (1¾in) diameter
Upholsterer's needle or long sharp darning needle
Strong thread

MEASUREMENTS:
35cm (14in) diameter

Yarn Notes

This cushion is made from Debbie Bliss Baby Cashmerino, a blend of 55 per cent merino wool, 33 per cent acrylic and 12 per cent cashmere, making it soft and luxurious but also very practical. There are 125m (137 yds) in a 50g (1¾oz) ball. There are a number of similar yarns on the market. This is lighter than a standard DK (8-ply) yarn but thicker than a fingering (4-ply), so if you do substitute another yarn, be sure to check the tension or your cushion cover may be a different size from the one shown here, and you will need a different sized cushion pad.

Round 14: 1 ch, 1 dc in 1st dc, 1 dc in each of next 5 dc, 2 dc in next dc, (1 dc in each of next 6 dc, 2 dc in next dc) 11 times; join with a ss to 1st dc of round (96 sts).

Round 15: 1 ch, 1 dc in each dc of previous round; join with a ss to 1st dc of round.

Round 16: 1 ch, 1 dc in 1st dc, 1 dc in each of next 6 dc, 2 dc in next dc, (1 dc in each of next 7 dc, 2 dc in next dc) 11 times; join with a ss to 1st dc of round (108 sts).

Round 17: 1 ch, 1 dc in each dc of previous round; join with a ss to 1st dc of round.

Round 18: 1 ch, 1 dc in 1st dc, 1 dc in each of next 7 dc, 2 dc in next dc, (1 dc in each of next 8 dc, 2 dc in next dc) 11 times; join with a ss to 1st dc of round (120 sts).

Round 19: 1 ch, 1 dc in each dc of previous round; join with a ss to 1st dc of round.

Round 20: 1 ch, 1 dc in 1st dc, 1 dc in each of next 8 dc, 2 dc in next dc, (1 dc in each of next 9 dc, 2 dc in next dc) 11 times; join with a ss to 1st dc of round (132 sts).

Round 21: 1 ch, 1 dc in each dc of previous round; join with a ss to 1st dc of round.

Round 22: 1 ch, 1 dc in 1st dc, 1 dc in each of next 9 dc, 2 dc in next dc, (1 dc in each of next 10 dc, 2 dc in next dc) 11 times; join with a ss to 1st dc of round (144 sts).

Round 23: 1 ch, 1 dc in each dc of previous round; join with a ss to 1st dc of round.

Round 24: 1 ch, 1 dc in 1st dc, 1 dc in each of next 10 dc, 2 dc in next dc, (1 dc in each of next 11 dc, 2 dc in next dc) 11 times; join with a ss to 1st dc of round (156 sts).

Round 25: 1 ch, 1 dc in each dc of previous round; join with a ss to 1st dc of round.

Round 26: 1 ch, 1 dc in 1st dc, 1 dc in each of next 11 dc, 2 dc in next dc, (1 dc in each of next 12 dc, 2 dc in next dc) 11 times; join with a ss to 1st dc of round (168 sts).

Round 27: 1 ch, 1 dc in each dc of previous round; join with a ss to 1st dc of round.

Round 28: 1 ch, 1 dc in 1st dc, 1 dc in each of next 12 dc, 2 dc in next dc, (1 dc in each of next 13 dc, 2 dc in next dc) 11 times; join with a ss to 1st dc of round (180 sts).

Round 29: 1 ch, 1 dc in each dc of previous round; join with a ss to 1st dc of round.

Round 30: 1 ch, 1 dc in 1st dc, 1 dc in each of next 13 dc, 2 dc in next dc, (1 dc in each of next 14 dc, 2 dc in next dc) 11 times; join with a ss to 1st dc of round (192 sts).

Round 31: 1 ch, 1 dc in each dc of previous round; join with a ss to 1st dc of round.

Round 32: 1 ch, 1 dc in 1st dc, 1 dc in each of next 14 dc, 2 dc in next dc, (1 dc in each of next 15 dc, 2 dc in next dc) 11 times; join with a ss to 1st dc of round (204 sts).

Round 33: 1 ch, 1 dc in each dc of previous round; join with a ss to 1st dc of round.

Round 34: 1 ch, 1 dc in 1st dc, 1 dc in each of next 15 dc, 2 dc in next dc, (1 dc in each of next 16 dc, 2 dc in next dc) 11 times; join with a ss to 1st dc of round (216 sts).

Round 35: 1 ch, 1 dc in each dc of previous round; join with a ss to 1st dc of round; cut A and join in B.

Round 36: 1 ch, 1 dc in 1st dc, 1 dc in each of next 16 dc, 2 dc in next dc, (1 dc in each of next 17 dc, 2 dc in next dc) 11 times; join with a ss to 1st dc of round (228 sts).

Round 37: 1 ch, 1 dc in each dc of previous round; join with a ss to 1st dc of round.

Round 38: 1 ch, 1 dc in 1st dc, 1 dc in each of next 17 dc, 2 dc in next dc, (1 dc in each of next 18 dc, 2 dc in next dc) 11 times; join with a ss to 1st dc of round (240 sts).

Round 39: 1 ch, 1 dc in each dc of previous round; join with a ss to 1st dc of round.

Cut yarn and fasten off.

Side 2
Follow instructions for Side 1 but use yarn C instead of yarn A; do not cut yarn at end of round.

Button covers (make two)
Foundation round: with 3.50mm (US E/4, UK 9) hook and yarn B, make a magic ring and work 1 ch, 6 dc in ring; join with a ss to 1st dc of round (6 sts).

Round 1: 1 ch (does not count as a stitch), 2 dc in each dc of previous round; join with a ss to 1st dc of round (12 sts).

Round 2: 1 ch, 2 dc in each dc of previous round; join with a ss to 1st dc of round (24 sts).

Round 3: 1 ch, 1 dc in each dc of previous round; join with a ss to 1st dc of round.

Round 4: as round 3.

Round 5: 1 ch, 1 dc in 1st dc, (dc2tog over next 2 dc, 1 dc in next dc) seven times, dc2tog over last 2 dc; join with a ss to 1st dc of round (16 sts).

Cut yarn. Leaving a tail, and fasten off.

Making up
Place the two pieces together, right sides out, lining up the edges. Join, stitch by stitch, with dc and yarn B, inserting the hook into one loop only on both edges. When seam is two-thirds complete, insert the cushion pad and continue joining the two edges; fasten off and weave in tails of yarn.

For the covered buttons, thread the tail of yarn into a tapestry needle and pass the needle in and out of the stitch loops all around the edge of the Button Cover. Repeat with the second Button Cover. Place a button inside each of the Button Covers and pull up the yarn tails to enclose the buttons; fasten off each yarn tail firmly.

Thread an upholsterer's needle or long sharp needle with strong thread and fasten the thread securely to the centre of one side of the cushion cover, then take the needle right through the cushion at this centre point, through the shank of one of the covered buttons, back through to the other side of the cushion, then through the shank of the second button and back through the cushion at the same point. Pull tightly on the thread to create a dimple in the cushion, take the needle back through the button shank, back through the cushion and through the other button shank, then fasten off the thread securely behind the button.

Make two covered buttons and place one on each side of the cushion, linked by strong thread stitched right through the centre of the pad. You will need a sharp upholsterer's needle or darning needle long enough to pass through the cushion pad – and you may need a pair of pliers to help pull the needle through the stuffing.

The red double crochet seam creates an attractive ridged feature around the circumference of the cushion.

Spike

Colour and texture combine to make a cushion to fit all kinds of situations: bedroom, living room, kitchen or conservatory. Crocheted in sunny citrus colours, it adds a hot splash to a neutral room scheme.

CUSHION PATTERN

This cushion is worked in one piece, with buttonholes worked into the last two rows. It is worked in a striped stitch with spikes and colour changes after every two rows. To work a tr-spike, work 1 tr, inserting the hook into the next dc in the row below. There is no need to cut the yarns after each colour change, as those not in use can be carried up the side of the work and incorporated into the side seam at the making-up stage. If you prefer to cut and rejoin yarns, however, yarn tails can be used to stitch side seams – so be sure to leave a tail long enough for this purpose.

Tension

16 sts and 10 rows to 10cm (4in), measured over pattern using 4.00mm (US G/6, UK 8) hook and recommended yarn.

Front and Back

Foundation chain: using 4.00mm (US G/6, UK 8) hook and yarn A, make 66 ch.

Foundation row: 1 dc in 2nd ch from hook, 1 dc in each ch to end (65 sts).

Row 1: 1 ch (does not count as a st), 1 dc in each st of previous row, changing to yarn B in last part of last st; turn.

Row 2 (RS): 1 ch, 1 dc in 1st st, 1 dc in next st, *1 tr-spike, 1 dc in each of next 3 sts; rep from * to last 3 sts, 1 tr-spike, 1 dc in each of last 2 sts; turn.

Row 3: 1 ch (does not count as a st), 1 dc in each st of previous row, changing back to yarn A in last part of last st; turn.

Row 4: 1 ch, 1 dc in each of 1st 4 dc, *1 tr-spike, 1 dc in each of next 3 sts; rep from * to last st, 1 dc in last st; turn.

Row 5: 1 ch (does not count as a st), 1 dc in each st of previous row, changing to yarn C in last part of last st; turn.

Row 6: 1 ch, 1 dc in 1st st, 1 dc in next st, *1 tr-spike, 1 dc in each of next 3 sts; rep from * to last 3 sts, 1 tr-spike, 1 dc in each of last 2 sts; turn.

Row 7: 1 ch (does not count as a st), 1 dc in each st of previous row, changing back to yarn A in last part of last st; turn.

Row 8: 1 ch, 1 dc in each of 1st 4 dc, *1 tr-spike, 1 dc in each of next 3 sts; rep from * to last st, 1 dc in last st; turn.

EQUIPMENT

YARN:
100 per cent wool DK (8-ply) yarn, 4 x 50g (1¾oz) balls in orange (A) and 2 x 50g (1¾oz) balls each in red (B), yellow (C) and pink (D)

HOOK:
4.00mm (US G/6, UK 8)

CUSHION PAD:
Square, 40 x 40cm (16 x 16in)

OTHER ITEMS:
5 round buttons, 2cm (¾in) diameter

MEASUREMENTS
40 x 40cm (16 x 16in)

Yarn Notes

This cushion has been made using Patons Fairytale Dreamtime DK, a pure wool DK (8-ply) yarn marketed as a baby yarn, so it has a very soft feel. There are 90m (98½ yds) in a 50g (1¾oz) ball. If you substititue another yarn, choose a pure wool standard DK (8-ply).

Row 9: 1 ch, 1 dc in each st of previous row, changing to yarn D in last part of last st; turn.

Row 10: 1 ch, 1 dc in 1st st, 1 dc in next st, *1 tr-spike, 1 dc in each of next 3 sts; rep from * to last 3 sts, 1 tr-spike, 1 dc in each of last 2 sts; turn.

Row 11: 1 ch, 1 dc in each st of previous row, changing back to yarn A in last part of last st; turn.

Row 12: 1 ch, 1 dc in each of 1st 4 dc, *1 tr-spike, 1 dc in each of next 3 sts; rep from * to last st, 1 dc in last st; turn.

Row 13: 1 ch, 1 dc in each st of previous row, changing to yarn B in last part of last st; turn.

Rep rows 2–13 13 times, then rows 2–11 once more; cut all yarns apart from A and continue in A.

Next row: 1 ch, 1 dc in each of 1st 4 dc, *1 tr-spike, 1 dc in each of next 3 sts; rep from * to last st, 1 dc in last st; turn.

Next row (buttonholes): 1 ch, 1 dc in each of 1st 7 sts, 3 ch, (miss 3 sts, 1 dc in each of next 9 sts, 3 ch) four times, miss 3 sts, 1 dc in each st to end of row.

Next row: 1 ch, 1 dc in each dc of previous row and 3 dc in each 3-ch sp.

Cut yarn and fasten off.

Making up

Place the cover right side up on the work surface and fold the end with the buttonholes over by 22cm (9in) and the other end over by 31cm (12½in), so that it overlaps. Check that the overall length of the cover is now 40cm (16in); adjust if necessary. Pin the sides together, then stitch seam in backstitch. Turn right sides out.

Stitch the buttons in place, to correspond with the buttonholes.

Overlap the edges of the cushion cover in the centre back. When you stitch the seams, using backstitch, pay particular attention to the sections where the pieces overlap, as you will be stitching through three layers of fabric.

Make sure the buttons you choose are the right size for the buttonholes. Buttons that are too small will slip out, while buttons that are too big may stretch and distort the buttonholes.

Long stitches worked into rows below form decorative 'spikes' and break up a simple striped pattern into something more unusual and visually interesting.

Love

A heart-shaped cushion makes an ideal love token to make for someone special: not only is gorgeous and colourful, it is a lasting reminder of the person who took the time and trouble to make it.

CUSHION PATTERN

This cushion is worked in rows of half treble crochet. The colourwork details are worked following a chart and using the intarsia method, see below. Each coloured square on the chart represents a stitch. Each colour change is done in the last stage of the previous stitch. Colours not in use are carried at the back of the work. Where there is a large block of colour (more than three stitches in a row), it is advisable to use a separate length of yarn, wound on to a bobbin, to prevent too much stranding.

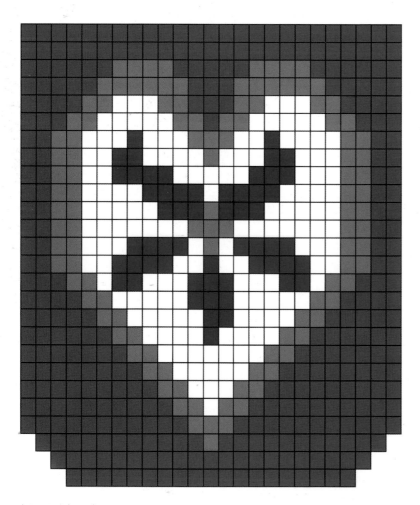

Intarsia colour chart.

EQUIPMENT

YARN:

100 per cent extra fine merino wool superwash DK (8-ply) yarn, 2 x 50g (1¾oz) balls in fuchsia (A) and 1 x 50g (1¾oz) ball each in mauve (B), ecru (C) and scarlet (D)

HOOK:

3.75mm (US F/5, UK 8 or 9)

CUSHION PAD:

Heart-shaped, 30cm (12in) tall and 28cm (11in) wide

This cushion cover has been designed to fit a pre-made heart-shaped cushion pad. If you cannot buy a heart-shaped pad of the correct dimensions, use the finished cover to cut a template, and make your own. You will find instructions for making cushion pads on pages 12–13.

OTHER ITEMS:

Tapestry needle

MEASUREMENTS:

28cm (11in) at widest point

Yarn Notes

A soft pure wool yarn is ideal for this little cushion, which has been made using Debbie Bliss Rialto, 100 per cent extra fine merino wool. There are 105m (115 yds) in a 50g (1¾oz) ball. You could choose to substitute another standard DK (8-ply) weight yarn.

Tension

17 sts and 12 rows to 10cm (4in), measured over rows of htr using 3.75mm (US F/5, UK 8 or 9) hook and recommended yarn.

Back

Foundation chain: with 3.75mm (US F/5, UK 8 or 9) hook and yarn A, make 3 ch.

Foundation row (RS): 2 htr in 3rd ch from hook; turn (3 sts).

Row 1: 2 ch (counts as 1 htr), 1 htr in 1st st, 1 htr in next st, 2 htr in turning ch; turn (5 sts).

Row 2: 2 ch, 1 htr in 1st st, 1 htr in each htr of previous row, 2 htr in turning ch.

Rep row 2 20 times (45 sts).

Row 22: 2 ch, 1 htr in each htr of previous row, 1 htr in turning ch.

Rep row 22 13 times.

Shape top

Row 1: 2 ch, 1 htr in each of next 20 sts, htr2tog over next 2 sts; place marker in next st and turn (22 sts).

Row 2: 2 ch, 1 htr in each st to last 2 sts, htr2tog; turn (21 sts).

Row 3: 1 ch (does not count as a st), htr2tog over 1st 2 sts, 1 htr in each st to last 2 sts, htr2tog; turn.

Rep row 3 three times more (13 sts); cut yarn and fasten off.

Rejoin yarn to centre (marked) st, work htr2tog over this st and next st, 1 htr in each st to end, including turning ch; turn (22 sts).

Next row: 1 ch, htr2tog over 1st 2 sts, 1 htr in each st to end.

Complete to match first side.

Front

Work following instructions for Back, incorporating charted design, starting on row 8.

Making up

With right sides together, stitch Front to Back in backstitch (see page 14), leaving a gap of approximately 15cm (6in) on one of the sloping sides. Turn right sides out and insert cushion pad, then slipstitch edges together neatly.

The colourful flower motif is worked using the intarsia method. You will find the stitch chart on page 74.

To create a neat intarsia motif, work with separate small balls or bobbins of each yarn colour. When changing colour, twist yarns together on the wrong side of the work. Afterwards, weave in yarn ends carefully on the wrong side.

Use a backstitch seam to join Front and Back sections of the cushion cover. Make sure the seam is firmly stitched, so that shaped edges look neat when the cover is turned right sides out.

Pool

Inspired by the ripples on the surface of water in a pool, the concentric circles are worked in close-matched colours. A firm, round cushion like this is perfect to top a stool or chair.

CUSHION PATTERN

This cushion is worked in rounds of double crochet; the scalloped edging is worked into the edge of the circle.

Tension

21 sts and 19 rows to 10cm (4in) measured over rows of dc using 4.00mm (US G/6, UK 8) hook and recommended yarn.

Side 1

Foundation round: with 4.00mm (US G/6, UK 8) hook and yarn A, make a magic ring and work 1 ch, 6 dc in ring; join with a ss to 1st dc of round (6 sts).

Round 1: 1 ch (does not count as a stitch), 2 dc in each dc of previous round; join with a ss to 1st dc of round (12 sts).

Round 2: 1 ch, 2 dc in each dc of previous round; join with a ss to 1st dc of round (24 sts).

Round 3: 1 ch, 1 dc in each dc of previous round; join with a ss to 1st dc of round; cut A and join in B.

Round 4: 1 ch, 1 dc in 1st dc, 2 dc in next dc, (1 dc in next dc, 2 dc in next dc) 11 times; join with a ss to 1st dc of round (36 sts).

Round 5: 1 ch, 1 dc in each dc of previous round; join with a ss to 1st dc of round.

Round 6: 1 ch, 1 dc in 1st dc, 1 dc in next dc, 2 dc in next dc, (1 dc in each of next 2 dc, 2 dc in next dc) 11 times; join with a ss to 1st dc of round (48 sts).

Round 7: 1 ch, 1 dc in each dc of previous round; join with a ss to 1st dc of round; cut B and join in C.

Round 8: 1 ch, 1 dc in 1st dc, 1 dc in each of next 2 dc, 2 dc in next dc, (1 dc in each of next 3 dc, 2 dc in next dc) 11 times; join with a ss to 1st dc of round (60 sts).

Round 9: 1 ch, 1 dc in each dc of previous round; join with a ss to 1st dc of round.

Round 10: 1 ch, 1 dc in 1st dc, 1 dc in each of next 3 dc, 2 dc in next dc, (1 dc in each of next 4 dc, 2 dc in next dc) 11 times; join with a ss to 1st dc of round (72 sts).

Round 11: 1 ch, 1 dc in each dc of previous round; join with a ss to 1st dc of round; cut C and join in D.

Round 12: 1 ch, 1 dc in 1st dc, 1 dc in each of next 4 dc, 2 dc in next dc, (1 dc in each of next 5 dc, 2 dc in next dc) 11 times; join with a ss to 1st dc of round (84 sts).

Round 13: 1 ch, 1 dc in each dc of previous round; join with a ss to 1st dc of round.

EQUIPMENT

YARN:
Pure wool DK (8-ply) yarn, 2 x 50g (1¾oz) balls in indigo (A), 1 x 50g (1¾oz) ball each in sage green (B), grey-green (C), cobalt blue (D) and plum (E)

HOOK:
4.00mm (US G/6, UK 8)

CUSHION PAD:
Round, 40cm (16in) diameter, with 5cm (2in) gusset

MEASUREMENTS:
38cm (15in) diameter, not including scalloped edge

Yarn Notes

This cushion has been made using Rowan 100 per cent wool DK, chosen for its soft yet durable quality and excellent range of colours. Toning shades of green and blue have been used here but you could choose your own palette of five colours.

Create the scalloped borders in different colours, to give your cushion a definite Front and Back.

Round 14: 1 ch, 1 dc in 1st dc, 1 dc in each of next 5 dc, 2 dc in next dc, (1 dc in each of next 6 dc, 2 dc in next dc) 11 times; join with a ss to 1st dc of round (96 sts).

Round 15: 1 ch, 1 dc in each dc of previous round; join with a ss to 1st dc of round; cut D and join in E.

Round 16: 1 ch, 1 dc in 1st dc, 1 dc in each of next 6 dc, 2 dc in next dc, (1 dc in each of next 7 dc, 2 dc in next dc) 11 times; join with a ss to 1st dc of round (108 sts).

Round 17: 1 ch, 1 dc in each dc of previous round; join with a ss to 1st dc of round.

Round 18: 1 ch, 1 dc in 1st dc, 1 dc in each of next 7 dc, 2 dc in next dc, (1 dc in each of next 8 dc, 2 dc in next dc) 11 times; join with a ss to 1st dc of round (120 sts).

Round 19: 1 ch, 1 dc in each dc of previous round; join with a ss to 1st dc of round; cut E and rejoin A.

Round 20: 1 ch, 1 dc in 1st dc, 1 dc in each of next 8 dc, 2 dc in next dc, (1 dc in each of next 9 dc, 2 dc in next dc) 11 times; join with a ss to 1st dc of round (132 sts).

Round 21: 1 ch, 1 dc in each dc of previous round; join with a ss to 1st dc of round.

Round 22: 1 ch, 1 dc in 1st dc, 1 dc in each of next 9 dc, 2 dc in next dc, (1 dc in each of next 10 dc, 2 dc in next dc) 11 times; join with a ss to 1st dc of round (144 sts).

Round 23: 1 ch, 1 dc in each dc of previous round; join with a ss to 1st dc of round; cut A and rejoin B.

Round 24: 1 ch, 1 dc in 1st dc, 1 dc in each of next 10 dc, 2 dc in next dc, (1 dc in each of next 11 dc, 2 dc in next dc) 11 times; join with a ss to 1st dc of round (156 sts).

Round 25: 1 ch, 1 dc in each dc of previous round; join with a ss to 1st dc of round.

Round 26: 1 ch, 1 dc in 1st dc, 1 dc in each of next 11 dc, 2 dc in next dc, (1 dc in each of next 12 dc, 2 dc in next dc) 11 times; join with a ss to 1st dc of round (168 sts).

Round 27: 1 ch, 1 dc in each dc of previous round; join with a ss to 1st dc of round; cut B and rejoin C.

Round 28: 1 ch, 1 dc in 1st dc, 1 dc in each of next 12 dc, 2 dc in next dc, (1 dc in each of next 13 dc, 2 dc in next dc) 11 times; join with a ss to 1st dc of round (180 sts).

Round 29: 1 ch, 1 dc in each dc of previous round; join with a ss to 1st dc of round.

Round 30: 1 ch, 1 dc in 1st dc, 1 dc in each of next 13 dc, 2 dc in next dc, (1 dc in each of next 14 dc, 2 dc in next dc) 11 times; join with a ss to 1st dc of round (192 sts).

Round 31: 1 ch, 1 dc in each dc of previous round; join with a ss to 1st dc of round; cut C and rejoin D.

Round 32: 1 ch, 1 dc in 1st dc, 1 dc in each of next 14 dc, 2 dc in next dc, (1 dc in each of next 15 dc, 2 dc in next dc) 11 times; join with a ss to 1st dc of round (204 sts).

Round 33: 1 ch, 1 dc in each dc of previous round; join with a ss to 1st dc of round.

Round 34: 1 ch, 1 dc in 1st dc, 1 dc in each of next 15 dc, 2 dc in next dc, (1 dc in each of next 16 dc, 2 dc in next dc) 11 times; join with a ss to 1st dc of round (216 sts).

Round 35: 1 ch, 1 dc in each dc of previous round; join with a ss to 1st dc of round; cut D and rejoin A.

Side 2

Follow instructions for side 1 but change colour sequence: start with yarn E, then change to D, then A, then B, then C, then E again, then D, then A, finishing with B.

Gusset

Foundation round: using 4.00mm (US G/6, UK 8) hook and yarn A, make 216 ch; join with a ss to 1st ch, to make a ring.

Round 1: 1 ch (does not count as a st), 1 dc in each ch; join with a ss to 1st dc of round (216 sts).

Round 2: 1 ch, 1 dc in each dc of previous round.

Rep round 2 nine times.

Cut yarn and fasten off.

Making up and borders

Place one edge of the gusset together with Side 1, right sides out, lining up edges. Using 4.00mm (US G/6, UK 8) hook and yarn E, join, stitch by stitch, with dc, inserting the hook into one loop only on both edges. When you reach the beginning, join with a ss to 1st dc of round, then work scalloped border as follows:

Round 1: 1 ch (does not count as a st), 1 dc in each of 1st 2 dc, *miss 2 dc, 6 tr in next dc, miss 2 dc, 1 dc in each of next 2 dc; rep from * to last 5 sts, miss 2 dc, 6 tr in next dc, miss 2 dc; join with a ss in 1st dc of round.

Cut yarn and fasten off.

Line up the edge of Side 2 with the other edge of the gusset and, using 4.00mm (US G/6, UK 8) hook and yarn C, join, stitch by stitch, with dc, inserting the hook into one loop only on both edges. When seam is two-thirds complete, insert the cushion pad and continue joining the two edges. When you reach the beginning, join with a ss to 1st dc of round, then work scalloped border, as before.

The circular Back and Front sections are joined with a narrow gusset. Fill this cover with a pad that is very slightly larger in diameter, as this will create a well-stuffed, firm cushion.

For a neat, decorative edge, the pieces are joined with double-crochet seams and the scalloped borders are worked into these seams.

Chicken

Made from a soft, supple bamboo yarn, this chicken cushion would not look out of place in a kitchen but would also make a delightful companion for a child or anyone who collects poultry-inspired items. The wedge shape makes this a really comfy neck pillow.

CUSHION PATTERN

This cushion is worked mainly in rows of double crochet.

Tension

21 sts and 24 rows to 10cm (4in), measured over rows of dc using 3.50mm (US E/4, UK 9) hook.

Base

Foundation chain: with 3.50mm (US E/4, UK 9) hook and A, make 26 ch.

Foundation row (RS): 1 dc in 2nd ch from hook, 1 dc in each ch to end; turn (25 sts).

Row 1: 1 ch (does not count as a st), 1 dc in each dc of previous row; turn.

Rep row 1 58 times.

Front

Row 1: inserting the hook into the front loop only of each st (for this row only), work 1 ch, 1 dc in each dc to end of round; turn.

*Row 2: 1 ch, dc2tog over 1st 2 sts, 1 dc in each dc to last 2 sts, dc2tog over last 2 sts; turn.

Row 3: 1 ch, 1 dc in each dc of previous row; turn.

Rows 4 and 5: as row 3.

Rep rows 2–5 nine times, then rows 2 and 3 once more (3 sts).

Cut yarn, leaving a tail, and fasten off.**

Back

With RS facing, rejoin yarn to opposite end of base and work 1 dc into each ch on foundation ch.

Follow instructions for Front from * to **.

Side 1

With RS facing and one of the long side edges of the base uppermost, join yarn to right-hand side.

Foundation row: work 50 dc, evenly spaced, along side of base, inserting hook into row ends; turn.

Row 1: 1 ch, 1 dc in each dc of previous row; turn.

Rep row 1 40 times.

Cut yarn, leaving a tail, and fasten off.

EQUIPMENT

YARN:
Bamboo-wool blend DK (8-ply) yarn, 6 x 50g (1¾oz) balls in orange (A) and 1 x 50g (1¾oz) ball in yellow (B)

HOOK:
3.50mm (US E/4, UK 9)

CUSHION PAD:
Custom-made, wedge-shaped (see Making Cushion Pads, pages 12–13 and Cushion Pad, on page 84), filled with polyester toy stuffing

OTHER ITEMS:
Tapestry needle
Polyester toy stuffing
2 round buttons, 2.5cm (1in) diameter
Sewing needle
Black thread

MEASUREMENTS:
26cm (10½in) long, 11.5cm (4½in) wide (at widest point) and 28cm (11in) tall, including head

Yarn Notes

This cushion has been made using Sirdar Snuggly Baby Bamboo, which is a blend of 80 per cent bamboo-sourced viscose and 20 per cent wool, creating a soft fabric with a slight stretch. There are 95m (104 yds) in a 50g (1¾oz) ball.

Side 2

With RS facing, turn work so that opposite long edge of base is uppermost, then work to match Side 1.

Wing (make two)

Foundation chain: using 3.50mm (US E/4, UK 9) hook and yarn B, make 3 ch.

Foundation row: 1 dc in 2nd ch from hook, 1 dc in next ch; turn (2 sts).

Row 1: 1 ch (does not count as a st), 2 dc in 1st dc, 2 dc in next dc; turn (4 sts).

Row 2: 1 ch, 1 dc in each dc of previous row; turn.

Row 3: 1 ch, 2 dc in 1st dc, 1 dc in each dc to last dc, 2 dc in last dc; turn.

Rep rows 2 and 3 three times more (12 sts).

Row 10: 1 ch, 1 dc in each dc of previous row; turn.

Rep row 10 eight times more.

Row 19: 1 ch, 1 dc in 1st dc, dc2tog over next 2 dc, 1 dc in each of next 6 dc, dc2tog over next 2 dc, 1 dc in last dc; turn (10 sts).

Row 20: 1 ch, 1 dc in 1st dc, dc2tog over next 2 dc, 1 dc in each of next 4 dc, dc2tog, 1 dc in last dc; turn (8 sts).

Row 21: 1 ch, 1 dc in 1st dc, dc2tog, 1 dc in each of next 2 dc, dc2tog, 1 dc in last dc; turn (6 sts).

Row 22: 1 ch, 1 dc in 1st dc, (dc2tog) twice, 1 dc in last dc (4 sts). Cut yarn, leaving a tail, and fasten off.

If you are making the cushion for a child, make sure you stitch all the components firmly in place.

Neck ruff

Foundation chain: using 3.50mm (US E/4, UK 9) hook and B, make 30 ch; join with a ss to 1st ch to form a ring.

Foundation row: 1 ch (does not count as a st), 1 dc in each ch to end of round; join with a ss to 1st dc of round (30 sts).

Round 1: 1 ch, 1 dc in each of 1st 4 dc, 2 dc in next dc, (1 dc in each of next 4 dc, 2 dc in next dc) five times (36 sts).

Round 2: *8 ch, 1 dc in 2nd ch from hook, 1 dc in next ch, (1 htr in next ch) twice, (1 tr in next ch) three times, miss 1 ch, ss in each of next 2 dc; rep from * to end of round; join with a ss to base of 8 ch at beg of round.

Cut yarn and fasten off.

Crest

Foundation chain: using 3.50mm (US E/4, UK 9) hook and B, make 14 ch.

Row 1: 1 dc in 2nd ch from hook, *(1 htr, 1 tr) in next ch, (1 dtr, 4 ch, 1 ss) in next ch, 1 dc in next ch; rep from * three times more.

Cut yarn, leaving a tail, and fasten off.

Short tail feather (make three)

Foundation chain: using 3.50mm (US E/4, UK 9) hook and B, make 4 ch.

Foundation row: 1 dc in 2nd ch from hook, 1 dc in each of next 2 ch; turn (3 sts).

Row 1: 1 ch (does not count as a st), 2 dc in 1st dc, 1 dc in next dc, 2 dc in last dc; turn (5 sts).

Row 2: 1 ch, 1 dc in each dc of previous row; turn.

Row 3: 1 ch, 2 dc in 1st dc, 1 dc in each dc to last dc, 2 dc in last dc; turn (7 sts).

Row 4: 1 ch, 1 dc in each dc of previous row; turn.

Rep row 4 11 times more.

Row 16: 1 ch, 1 dc in 1st dc, dc2tog over next 2 dc, 1 dc in next dc, dc2tog over next 2 dc, 1 dc in last dc (5 sts).

Row 17: 1 ch, dc2tog, 1 dc in next dc, dc2tog (3 sts).

Cut yarn and fasten off.

Medium tail feather (make two)

Follow pattern for Short tail feather to end of row 4.

Rep row 4 15 times more.

Continue following pattern for Short tail feather from row 16 to end.

Eye (make two)

Foundation round: with 3.50mm (US E/4, UK 9) hook and yarn B, make a magic ring and work 1 ch, 6 dc in ring; join with a ss to 1st dc of round (6 sts).

Round 1: 1 ch (does not count as a stitch), 2 dc in each dc of previous round; join with a ss to 1st dc of round (12 sts).

Round 2: 1 ch, 2 dc in each dc of previous round; join with a ss to 1st dc of round (24 sts).

Cut yarn, leaving a tail, and fasten off.

Beak

Foundation round: with 3.50mm (US E/4, UK 9) hook and yarn B, make a magic ring and work 1 ch, 6 dc in ring; join with a ss to 1st dc of round (6 sts).

Round 1: 1 ch (does not count as a stitch), 1 dc in 1st dc, 2 dc in next dc, (1 dc in next dc, 2 dc in next dc) twice; join with a ss to 1st dc of round (9 sts).

Round 2: 1 ch, 1 dc in each of first 2 dc, 2 dc in next dc, (1 dc in each of next 2 dc, 2 dc in next dc) twice; join with a ss to 1st dc of round (12 sts).

Round 3: 1 ch, 1 dc in each dc of previous round; join with a ss to 1st dc of round.

Rep round 3 three times more.

Cut yarn and fasten off.

Cushion Pad

Use the body section as a pattern for a wedge-shaped cushion pad. Lay the crocheted piece flat on a piece of fabric and draw all round. Add a 1cm (½in) seam allowance, cut out fabric and stitch side seams. Clip corners and turn right sides out. Stuff firmly with polyester toy filling, then tuck in 1cm (½in) on each top edge and oversew together along folds.

Making up

Using tails of yarn, and placing right sides together, stitch the four side seams in backstitch. Turn right sides out and stitch wings in place, one on each side. Stitch the base of each tail feather to the top (pointed) end of the back, on the inside. Place the cushion pad inside. Starting from the tail end, stitch the top seam using either the oversewing or flat seam method (see pages 15 and 16), stopping when you reach 13 sts from front end. Fasten off.

Head

Round 1: rejoin ball of orange yarn to this point, work 1 ch, then inserting the hook into the back loop only of each st, work 1 dc in each of 13 sts along top edge of left-hand

Secure the tail feathers to the inside before stitching the seam along the top of the Chicken.

side to front, 1 dc in each of 4 sts across top of front, 1 dc in each of 13 sts along top edge of right-hand side; join with a ss to 1st dc of round (30 sts).

Round 2: 1 ch, 1 dc in each dc of previous round; join with a ss to 1st dc of round.

Rep round 2 11 times more.

Round 14: 1 ch, 1 dc in 1st dc, 1 dc in each of next 3 dc, (dc2tog over next 2 dc, 1 dc in each of next 4 dc) four times, dc2tog over last 2 dc; join with a ss to 1st dc of round (25 sts).

Round 15: 1 ch, 1 dc in each dc of previous round; join with a ss to 1st dc of round.

Round 16: 1 ch, 1 dc in 1st dc, 1 dc in each of next 2 dc, (dc2tog over next 2 dc, 1 dc in each of next 3 dc) four times, dc2tog over last 2 dc; join with a ss to 1st dc of round (20 sts).

Round 17: 1 ch, 1 dc in 1st dc, 1 dc next dc, (dc2tog over next 2 dc, 1 dc in each of next 2 dc) four times, dc2tog over last 2 dc; join with a ss to 1st dc of round (15 sts).

Round 18: 1 ch, 1 dc in 1st dc, (dc2tog over next 2 dc, 1 dc in next dc) four times, dc2tog over last 2 dc; join with a ss to 1st dc of round (10 sts).

Cut yarn, leaving a tail, but do not fasten off.

Stitch eyes in place on head; sew a button in the centre of each crocheted eye piece, using black thread.

Stuff head. Thread yarn tail at top of head into tapestry needle and pass the needle in and out of the stitch loops on the last round. Pull yarn tail to close gap and enclose stuffing, then fasten off securely. Stitch crest in place along top of head. Slip Neck ruff over head and sew in place, stitch by stitch, to expose stitch loops around base of head. Stuff beak and stitch in place.

Patch

Granny squares are a perennial favourite: here, using a variegated yarn for the centre of each square avoids having to change colour, so there are fewer ends to weave in. Use this cushion, made from fingering (4-ply) alpaca sock yarn, wherever you want to add a soft, cosy touch.

CUSHION PATTERN

This cushion is made up from 18 granny squares with a complementary border. This pattern is a variation of the granny square given on pages 54–57. Because it is worked in one colour, I find it easier to turn the work after each round, so that you can work into the next space more easily. The other difference is that each 'petal' is made up of two trebles, rather than three; this uses slightly less yarn, which is useful when working with more expensive yarns.

Tension

Using the recommended yarn and a 3.00mm (US C/2 or D/3, UK 11) hook, one granny square measures 7cm (2¾in).

Granny squares (make 18)

Foundation chain: with 3.00mm (US C/2 or D/3, UK 11) hook and yarn A, make 4 ch, join with a ss to 1st ch to make a ring.

Round 1: 3 ch (counts as 1 tr), 1 tr into ring, 3 ch, (2 tr in ring, 3 ch) three times, join with ss to 3rd of 3 ch; turn.

Round 2: ss into next 3-ch sp, 3 ch (counts as 1 tr), 1 tr into sp, 3 ch, 2 tr into same sp, 2 ch, *(2 tr, 3 ch, 2 tr) in next 3-ch sp, 2 ch; rep from * twice more; join with a ss to 3rd of 3 ch; turn.

Round 3: ss into next 2-ch sp, 3 ch (counts as 1 tr), 1 tr into sp, *2 ch, (2 tr, 3 ch, 2 tr) in next 3-ch sp, 2 ch, 2 tr in next 2-ch sp; rep from * twice more, 2 ch, (2 tr, 3 ch, 2 tr) in last 3-ch sp, 2 ch; join with a ss to 3rd of 3 tr as beg of round. Cut yarn and fasten off.

Round 4: join yarn B to any 3-ch corner sp and work 3 ch (counts as 1 tr), 1 tr into sp, *(2 ch, 2 tr in next 2-ch sp) twice, 2 ch, (2 tr, 3 ch, 2 tr) in next 3-ch sp, rep from * twice more, *(2 ch, 2 tr in next 2-ch sp) twice, 2 ch, 2 tr in 1st 3-ch sp, 3 ch; join with a ss to 3rd of 3 ch at beg of round.

EQUIPMENT

YARN:
Alpaca, silk and cashmere blend fingering (4-ply) sock yarn, 100g (3½oz) each in variegated shades (A), dark blue (B), pale green (C) and pink (D)

HOOK:
3.00mm (US C/2 or D/3, UK 11)

CUSHION PAD:
Square, 30 x 30cm (12 x 12in), covered with cotton fabric in green or other contrast colour

MEASUREMENTS:
30 x 30cm (12 x 12in)

Yarn Notes

This cushion has been made using Angelus 4-ply, a luxurious blend of 70 per cent baby alpaca, 20 per cent silk and 10 per cent cashmere from The Natural Dye Studio, in the south-west of England. The centre of each granny square has been crocheted in a variegated mix of yellow, pink, blue and green. There are many luxury fingering (4-ply) sock yarns on the market, so if you do decide on a different yarn, check your tension.

Making up and borders

Join nine squares to make the Front and the same for the Back. Use a flat seaming technique for the neatest finish (see page 16). Work a border of 1 round, using yarn C, working (2 tr, 3 ch, 2 tr) in each corner sp and (2 tr, 2 ch) in each sp along straight edges, in a similar way to round 4. Cut yarn C, join yarn D to any 3-ch corner sp and work five further rounds, once again working 2 tr, 3 ch, 2 tr in each 3-ch corner sp and 2 tr, 2 ch in each 2-ch sp along straight edges.

To join the cushion cover, place Back and Front together, right sides out and using yarn D, work a row of dc all round (1 dc in each st and 3 dc in each corner), inserting hook through one loop only of each corresponding edge stitch on both pieces, creating a neat raised seam (see page 15). When the seam is three-quarters complete, insert the cushion pad and continue joining the two edges; fasten off and weave in tails of yarn.

> **Note:**
> As this cushion cover has holes, you will be able to see the cushion pad underneath, so make a simple cotton fabric cover in a contrasting colour, such as bright green.

Nine granny squares form an attractive centrepiece for the cushion, and a narrow border of pale green and wider border of pink create an attractive frame. Have fun experimenting with your own colour combinations.

Variegated yarns produce a multicoloured effect without the need for constant colour changes and leave fewer yarn ends to weave in at the making-up stage.

Use a plain yarn in a contrasting colour – like the dark blue used here – for the last round of each granny square, to create a balanced framework when the squares are joined together.

Boudoir

Here is an unashamedly feminine cushion that will delight any girl, young or old, who enjoys frills, flowers and all things pink and pretty. Place it on a bed or chair where the flower decoration can be displayed to its best advantage.

CUSHION PATTERN

This cushion is worked in rounds of double crochet. You will need to work increases on every other round to create the circular shape. The four-layered flower is also worked in the round, made separately and stitched in place at the making-up stage. The border is made in a similar way to the petals of the flower.

Tension

23 sts and 22 rows to 10cm (4in), measured over rows of double crochet, using 3.75mm (US F/5, UK 8 or 9) hook and the recommended yarn.

Front

Foundation round: with 3.75mm (US F/5, UK 8 or 9) hook and yarn A, make a magic ring and work 1 ch, 6 dc in ring; join with a ss to 1st dc of round (6 sts).

Round 1: 1 ch (does not count as a stitch), 2 dc in each dc of previous round; join with a ss to 1st dc of round (12 sts).

Round 2: 1 ch, 2 dc in each dc of previous round; join with a ss to 1st dc of round (24 sts).

Round 3 (and each odd-numbered round): 1 ch, 1 dc in each dc of previous round; join with a ss to 1st dc of round.

Round 4: 1 ch, 1 dc in 1st dc, 2 dc in next dc, (1 dc in next dc, 2 dc in next dc) 11 times; join with a ss to 1st dc of round (36 sts).

Round 6: 1 ch, 1 dc in each of 1st 2 dc, 2 dc in next dc, (1 dc in each of next 2 dc, 2 dc in next dc) 11 times; join with a ss to 1st dc of round (48 sts).

Round 8: 1 ch, 1 dc in each of 1st 3 dc, 2 dc in next dc, (1 dc in each of next 3 dc, 2 dc in next dc) 11 times; join with a ss to 1st dc of round (60 sts).

Round 10: 1 ch, 1 dc in each of 1st 4 dc, 2 dc in next dc, (1 dc in each of next 4 dc, 2 dc in next dc) 11 times; join with a ss to 1st dc of round (72 sts).

Round 12: 1 ch, 1 dc in each of 1st 5 dc, 2 dc in next dc, (1 dc in each of next 5 dc, 2 dc in next dc) 11 times; join with a ss to 1st dc of round (84 sts).

Round 14: 1 ch, 1 dc in each of 1st 6 dc, 2 dc in next dc, (1 dc in each of next 6 dc, 2 dc in next dc) 11 times; join with a ss to 1st dc of round (96 sts).

Round 16: 1 ch, 1 dc in each of 1st 7 dc, 2 dc in next dc, (1 dc in each of next 7 dc, 2 dc in next dc) 11 times; join with a ss to 1st dc of round (108 sts).

Round 18: 1 ch, 1 dc in each of 1st 8 dc, 2 dc in next dc, (1 dc in each of next 8 dc, 2 dc in next dc) 11 times; join with a ss to 1st dc of round (120 sts).

EQUIPMENT

YARN:
Wool-cashmere blend DK (8-ply) yarn, 2 x 50g (1¾oz) balls in ivory (A), 1 x 50g (1¾oz) ball each in palest pink (B), fuchsia (C) and bright pink (D)

HOOK:
3.75mm (US F/5, UK 8 or 9)

CUSHION PAD:
Round, 28cm (11in) diameter

OTHER ITEMS:
Tapestry needle

MEASUREMENTS:
28cm (11in) in diameter without border, 32cm (12¾in) in diameter including border

Yarn Notes

This cushion has been made using Sublime Baby Cashmere Merino Silk DK, a luxurious blend of 75 per cent merino wool, 20 per cent silk and 5 per cent cashmere. There are 116m (127 yds) in a 50g (1¾oz) ball and it is a standard DK (8-ply) weight, which means that you can substitute another DK (8-ply) yarn, if you wish.

Round 20: 1 ch, 1 dc in each of 1st 9 dc, 2 dc in next dc, (1 dc in each of next 9 dc, 2 dc in next dc) 11 times; join with a ss to 1st dc of round (132 sts).

Round 22: 1 ch, 1 dc in each of 1st 10 dc, 2 dc in next dc, (1 dc in each of next 10 dc, 2 dc in next dc) 11 times; join with a ss to 1st dc of round (144 sts).

Round 24: 1 ch, 1 dc in each of 1st 11 dc, 2 dc in next dc, (1 dc in each of next 11 dc, 2 dc in next dc) 11 times; join with a ss to 1st dc of round (156 sts).

Round 26: 1 ch, 1 dc in each of 1st 12 dc, 2 dc in next dc, (1 dc in each of next 12 dc, 2 dc in next dc) 11 times; join with a ss to 1st dc of round (168 sts).

Round 27: 1 ch, 1 dc in each dc of previous round; join with a ss to 1st dc of round.

Round 28: as round 27.

Cut yarn and fasten off.

Back

Follow instructions for Front.

Flower

Centre flower

Foundation chain: with 3.75mm (US F/5, UK 8 or 9) hook and yarn B, make 8 ch; join with a ss to 1st ch.

Round 1: 1 ch (does not count as a stitch), 16 dc into ring; join with a ss to 1st dc of round (16 sts).

Round 2: 5 ch (counts as 1 tr, 2 ch), miss next dc, (1 tr in next dc, 2 ch, miss 1 dc) seven times; join with a ss to 3rd of 5 ch.

Round 3: ss into next 2-ch sp, 1 ch, (1 dc, 1 htr, 1 tr, 1 htr, 1 dc) in each 2-ch sp; join with a ss to 1st dc of round; cut yarn.

Second layer

Round 1: with RS facing, join yarn C to base of any tr at back of centre flower; working behind each petal, 1 ch, 1 dc into base of same tr, (3 ch, miss 4 sts, 1 dc in base of next tr) seven times, 3 ch, join with a ss to 1st dc.

Round 2: ss into next 3-ch sp, 1 ch, (1 dc, 1 htr, 3 tr, 1 htr, 1 dc) into each 3-ch sp; join with a ss to 1st dc; cut yarn.

Third layer

Round 1: with RS facing, join yarn D to base of the middle tr in any 3 tr group from second layer at back of centre flower; working behind each petal, 1 ch, 1 dc into base of same tr, (5 ch, miss 6 sts, 1 dc in base of next tr) seven times, 5 ch, join with a ss to 1st dc.

Round 2: ss into next 5-ch sp, 1 ch, (1 dc, 1 htr, 5 tr, 1 htr, 1 dc) into each 5-ch sp; join with a ss to 1st dc; cut yarn.

Outer layer

Round 1: with RS facing, join yarn B to base of the middle tr in any 5 tr group from third layer at back of centre flower; working behind each petal, 1 ch, 1 dc into base of same tr, (7 ch, miss 8 sts, 1 dc in base of next tr) seven times, 7 ch, join with a ss to 1st dc.

Round 2: ss into next 7-ch sp, 1 ch, (1 dc, 1 htr, 7 tr, 1 htr, 1 dc) into each 7-ch sp; join with a ss to 1st dc; cut yarn.

Making up

Using tails of yarn, stitch the Flower in the centre of the cushion Front. Place Front and Back together, right sides out, lining up edges. Using 3.75mm (US F/5, UK 8 or 9) hook and yarn D, join, stitch by stitch, with dc, inserting the hook into one loop only on both edges. When seam is two-thirds complete, insert the cushion pad and continue joining the two edges.

Border

Round 1: 1 ch (does not count as a st), 1 dc in same place, 6 ch, miss 6 sts, 1 dc in next dc; rep from * to last 6 sts, 6 ch, miss 6 sts; join with a ss to 1st dc of round.

Round 2: ss into 1st 6-ch sp, (1 dc, 1 htr, 7 tr, 1 htr, 1 dc) into each 6-ch sp to end of round; join with a ss to 1st dc. Cut yarn and fasten off.

Weave in all remaining yarn ends.

The circular cushion provides the ideal background for this textured, layered flower, and the border complements it perfectly.

The scalloped 'petals' around the circumference of the cover are worked in a similar way to the flower petals in the cushion centre.

The four-tiered flower stands out in relief, raised up from the main part of the cover.

Tartan

Inspired by Scottish tartans, and using bright, bold colours, this firm, practical cushion would be right at home in a traditional interior, on top of a footstool by the fireplace.

CUSHION PATTERN

This cushion is worked in one piece, in rows of double crochet, with occasional one-row stripes and rectangles of contrast colours worked using the intarsia method. You will need to wind small amounts of yarn on to bobbins and twist yarns together on the wrong side of the work at each colour change. Additional lines are added at the making-up stage, embroidered in chain stitch.

Tension

19 sts and 22 rows to 10cm (4in), measured over rows of dc using 4.00mm (US G/6, UK 8) hook and the recommended yarn.

Front and Back

Foundation chain: using 4.00mm (US G/6, UK 8) hook and A, make 153 ch.

Foundation row: 1 dc in 2nd ch from hook, 1 dc in each ch to end (152 sts).

Row 1 (WS): 1 ch (does not count as a st), 1 dc in each dc to end; turn.

Rep row 1 six times more; do not cut yarn A but join in B.

Row 8: using B, 1 ch (does not count as a st), 1 dc in each dc to end; cut yarn; do not turn but return to beg of row and pick up yarn A.

Row 9 (RS): using A, 1 ch (does not count as a st), 1 dc in each dc to end; turn.

Rep row 9 five times more; rejoin yarn B.

*Row 15: using yarn B, 1 ch, 1 dc in 1st dc, (1 dc in each of next 15 dc using B, changing to yarn A in last part of last st, 1 dc in each of next 15 dc using A, changing to yarn B in last part of last st) four times; 1 dc in each of next 15 dc using B, changing in yarn A in last part of last st, 1 dc in each of next 15 dc using A; turn.

Row 16: using yarn A, 1 ch, 1 dc in 1st dc, (1 dc in each of next 15 dc using A, changing to yarn B in last part of last st, 1 dc in each of next 15 dc using B, joining in yarn A in last part of last st) four times; 1 dc in each of next 15 dc using A, joining in yarn B in last part of last st, 1 dc in each of next 15 dc using B; turn.

Rep rows 15 and 16 twice more; do not cut A and B but join in C.

Row 21: using C, 1 ch (does not count as a st), 1 dc in each dc to end; cut yarn; do not turn but return to beg of row and pick up yarn B.

Row 22 (RS): as row 15.

Row 23: as row 16.

Equipment

YARN:
Acrylic and nylon double crepe DK (8-ply) yarn, 4 x 50g balls in cherry red (A) and 1 x 50g ball each in royal blue (B), white (C) and bottle green (D)

HOOK:
4.00mm (US G/6, UK 8)

CUSHION PAD:
Rectangular, 43 x 33cm (17 x 13 in)

OTHER ITEMS:
30cm (12in) zip (red, white or royal blue)
Tapestry needle
Sewing thread, red

MEASUREMENTS:
40 x 30cm (16 x 12in)

Yarn Notes

This cushion has been made using Sirdar Wash 'n' Wear Double Crepe DK, a hard-wearing, practical yarn made from 55 per cent acrylic and 45 per cent nylon, that can be machine washed and tumble-dried and is available in a good range of colours. There are 135m (148 yds) in a 50g (1¾oz) ball. A crepe yarn such as this, which is firmly twisted, produces a crisp fabric with good stitch definition. As this yarn is a standard DK (8-ply) weight, you could substitute almost any standard DK (8-ply) yarn.

Rep rows 22 and 23 twice more; cut yarn B.

Row 28: using yarn A, 1 ch (does not count as a st), 1 dc in each dc to end; turn.

Rep row 1 five times more; do not cut yarn A but join in D.

Row 34: using D, 1 ch (does not count as a st), 1 dc in each dc to end; cut yarn; do not turn but return to beg of row and pick up yarn A.

Row 35 (RS): using A, 1 ch (does not count as a st), 1 dc in each dc to end; turn.**

Rep row 35 five times more; rejoin yarn D.

Rep from * to ** but substituting yarn D for yarn B in rows 15–27 and substituting yarn B for yarn D in row 34.

Rep row 35 five times more.

Cut yarn and fasten off.

Making up

With RS facing, thread a tapestry needle with a length of yarn C and stitch vertical lines of chain stitch up through the centre of each rectangle, then horizontally along the rows on either side of the rectangular blocks. Stitch additional vertical rows of chain stitch halfway between the blocks, using yarns B and D (see top tip box).

Pin one side of the zip to the wrong side of one of the side edges and the other side of the zip to the other side edge, then stitch in place. Join the ends of the seam at either end of the zip, using yarn tails.

With wrong sides out, pin the long edges together; open zip, then stitch seams in backstitch.

Turn right sides out through zip; insert cushion pad and close zip.

TOP TIP

Surface embroidery is a great way of adding decorative details to a crochet fabric. Use a tapestry needle, with a blunt tip – not a darning needle, which might split and weaken the crocheted stitches – and thread it with a length of yarn. Work rows of chain stitches, following the vertical or horizontal lines of crochet stitches, to keep the lines straight.

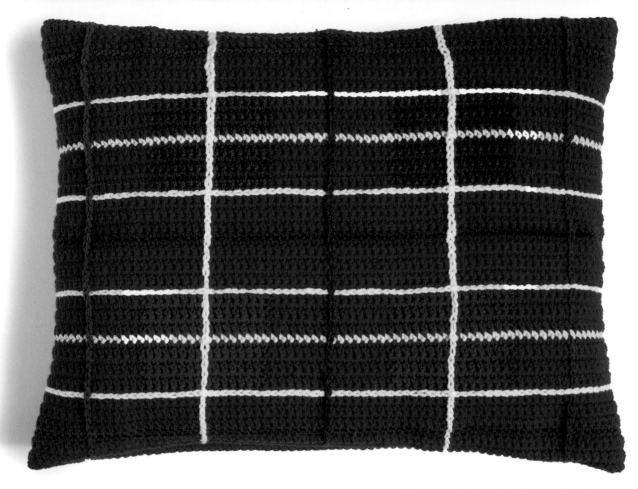

The square blocks, placed between broad stripes, are crocheted using the intarsia method. Narrow lines of chain stitch are then stitched vertically, through the centres of the intarsia blocks, and horizontally through the tops and bottoms of the blocks.

The zip is positioned across the whole width of the cushion. It needs to be stitched to the side edges of the crocheted fabric, using sewing thread, and this can be done by hand or machine.

97

Snail

Made from a fine tweedy yarn in five subtle colours, this small-scale cushion features a snail appliqué, made separately and stitched in place. Ideal for a child's room, it is both practical and whimsical.

CUSHION PATTERN

The main part of this cushion cover is worked in rows of double crochet, while the snail shell is worked in a spiral. The snail's body is worked in rounds. The snail trail is added afterwards, embroidered in chain stitch.

Tension

22 sts and 24 rows to 10cm (4in), measured over rows of dc using a 3.50mm (US E/4, UK 9) hook and the recommended yarn.

Front

Foundation chain: with 3.50mm (US E/4, UK 9) hook and yarn A, make 51 ch.

Foundation row (RS): 1 dc in 2nd ch from hook, 1 dc in each ch to end; turn (50 sts).

Row 1: 1 ch (does not count as st), 1 dc in each dc of previous row; turn.

Rep row 1 21 times more; cut yarn and join in yarn B, then rep row 1 23 times more.

Cut yarn and fasten off.

Border

Round 1: with RS facing, join yarn C to 1st dc of last row and work 1 ch (does not count as st), 2 dc in 1st dc, 1 dc in each dc to last st of row, 3 dc in last st; do not turn but work down side, working 40 dc, evenly spaced, into row ends; do not turn but work along foundation ch, working 3 dc in 1st ch, 1 dc in each ch to last ch of row, 3 dc in last ch, then work 40 dc into row ends on second side and 1 dc in same place as 1st 2 dc of round; join with a ss into 1st dc (188 sts).

Round 2: 1 ch, 2 dc in 1st dc, 1 dc in each dc of previous round, except 3 dc in each of rem 3 corner sts; finish with 1 dc in 1st corner (in same place as 1st dc of round); join with a ss into 1st dc (196 sts).

Round 3: as round 2 (204 sts).

Cut yarn and fasten off.

Back (in two halves)

*Foundation chain: with 3.50mm (US E/4, UK 9) hook and yarn A, make 51 ch.

Foundation row (RS): 1 dc in 2nd ch from hook, 1 dc in each ch to end; turn (50 sts).

Row 1: 1 ch (does not count as st), 1 dc in each dc of previous row; turn.

Rep row 1 21 times more.

Cut yarn and fasten off. **

EQUIPMENT

YARN:
Fingering (4-ply) tweed yarn, 1 x 50g (1¾oz) ball each of green (A), lavender (B), heather pink (C), pale grey (D) and white (E)

HOOK:
3.50mm (US E/4, UK 9)

CUSHION PAD:
Rectangular, 27 x 23cm (11 x 9in)

OTHER ITEMS:
20cm (8in) zip, green or lavender
Tapestry needle

MEASUREMENTS:
27 x 23cm (11 x 9in)

Yarn Notes

This cushion has been made using Rowan fine tweed, a fine fingering (4-ply) yarn spun from 100 per cent wool. A 50g (1¾oz) ball measures 90m (98½ yds) and the finished cover should be hand washed. If you are looking for an alternative, choose a natural wool tweed fingering (4-ply) yarn.

Rep from * to ** but using yarn B.

Pin the zip to the top (last row) of the first half and the base (foundation chain) of the second half, then stitch in place. Join the ends of the two halves at either end of the zip, using yarn tails.

Border

Complete as for Front.

Snail body

Foundation chain: with 3.50mm (US E/4, UK 9) hook and yarn C, make 31 ch.

Foundation round (RS): 1 dc in 2nd ch from hook, 1 dc in each of next 9 ch, 1 htr in each of next 10 ch, 1 tr in each of next 9 ch, 8 tr in next ch, then, working along opposite edge of foundation ch, 1 tr in each of next 10 ch, 1 htr in each of next 10 ch, 1 dc in each of next 9 ch, 2 dc in last ch, join with a ss to 1st dc of round.

Round 2: 1 ch (does not count as st), 1 dc in 1st dc, 1 dc in each of next 19 sts, 1 htr in each of next 10 sts, (2 htr in next st, 9 ch, 3 dc in 2nd ch from hook, ss in each of next 7 ch) twice, 2 htr in each of next 2 sts, (1 htr, 1 dc) in next st, 1 dc in each st to end; join with a ss to 1st dc of round.

Cut yarn and fasten off.

Snail shell (worked in a spiral)

Using yarn D, make a magic ring and work 1 ch, (1 dc, 1 htr, 2 tr) into ring; remove hook, leaving a loop (you may wish to place a stitch holder in the loop of yarn).

Join yarn E into ring and work 1 ch, (1 dc, 1 htr, 2 tr) into ring, then 2 tr in 1st dc, 2 tr into htr, (2 tr in next tr) twice; remove hook, leaving a loop, and pick up loop of D, then work 2 tr in next dc, 2 tr in htr, (2 tr in tr) 10 times; remove hook, leaving a loop, and pick up loop of E; work 2 tr in each of next 20 tr, 1 tr in next tr, 1 htr in next tr, 1 dc in next tr, join with a ss to next st, cut yarn and fasten off.

Pick up loop of D and work (1 tr in each of next 2 tr, 2 tr in next tr) until you reach the last 3 tr in yarn E, 1 tr in next tr, 1 htr in next tr, 1 dc in next tr, join with a ss to next st, cut yarn and fasten off.

Making up

Pin Snail Body across the join in the centre of the cushion Front and stitch in place using matching yarn. Pin the Snail Shell above the Body, then stitch in place. Thread the tapestry needle with a length of yarn E and embroider a snail trail in chain stitch, starting at the end of the Snail Body. Place the Front and Back of the cushion together and join all round edges using yarn C and double crochet (see page 17), inserting the hook into one loop each of every dc on the two edges.

There are several steps involved in creating this cushion. The main part of the cover is crocheted in one piece for the Front and two pieces for the Back. The snail's body and shell are made separately and stitched in place, then the snail trail is embroidered using chain stitch.

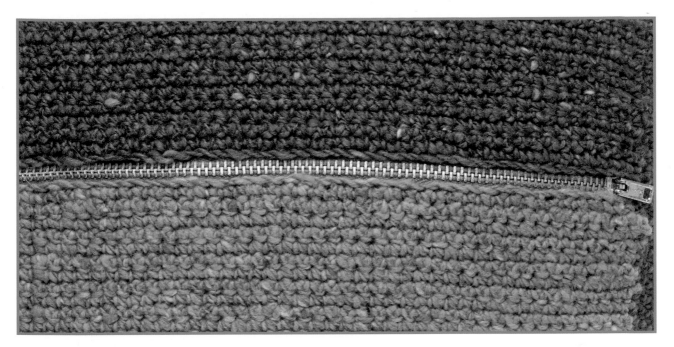

The back of the cushion cover features a zip across the centre, between the two pieces of crocheted fabric, which allows you to remove the cover for cleaning.

The snail trail is created with surface embroidery. Thread a tapestry needle with a length of yarn and embroider a meandering line in chain stitch.

Worked in the round, the snail shell is a neat two-colour spiral. This involves working with one colour at a time; you may wish to use stitch markers to help you keep track of the pattern.

Ruffle

A spiral ruffle of double trebles creates a richly textured, extravagant cushion that feels as good as it looks. Choose a bright colour, such as the variegated yellow used here, to create a flower-like effect.

CUSHION PATTERN

This cushion is worked in rounds of trebles, inserting the hook into the back loop only of every stitch, which creates a ridged effect. The ruffle is then worked into the stitch loops along this ridge.

Tension

21 sts and 19 rows to 10cm (4in), measured over rows of dc using 4.00mm (US G/6, UK 8) hook and the recommended yarn.

Front and Back (make two)

Work into back loops of stitches throughout.

Foundation round: using the 4.00 mm (US G/6, UK 8) hook, make a magic loop and work 1 ch (does not count as st) and 12 dc in loop.

Round 1: 3 ch (counts as 1 tr), 1 tr in same place, 2 tr in each st to end (24 sts); place a marker in last st and do not join to 1st st of round but continue working in a spiral.

Round 2: inserting hook into back loop only, (2 tr in next st, 1 tr in next st) 12 times (36 sts); place a marker in last st and do not join to 1st st of round but continue working in a spiral.

Round 3: (2 tr in next st, 1 tr in each of next 2 sts) 12 times (48 sts); place a marker in last st and do not join to 1st st of round but continue working in a spiral.

Round 4: (2 tr in next st, 1 tr in each of next 3 sts) 12 times (60 sts); place a marker in last st and do not join to 1st st of round but continue working in a spiral.

Round 5: (2 tr in next st, 1 tr in each of next 4 sts) 12 times (72 sts); place a marker in last st and do not join to 1st st of round but continue working in a spiral.

Round 6: (2 tr in next st, 1 tr in each of next 5 sts) 12 times (84 sts); place a marker in last st and do not join to 1st st of round but continue working in a spiral.

Round 7: (2 tr in next st, 1 tr in each of next 6 sts) 12 times (96 sts); do not join to 1st st of round but continue working in a spiral.

Round 8: (2 tr in next st, 1 tr in each of next 7 sts) 12 times (108 sts); do not join to 1st st of round but continue working in a spiral.

Round 9: (2 tr in next st, 1 tr in each of next 8 sts) 12 times (120 sts); do not join to 1st st of round but continue working in a spiral.

EQUIPMENT

YARN:
Pure superwash merino wool DK (8-ply) yarn, 2 x 115g (4oz) hanks in variegated yellow

HOOK:
4.00mm (US G/6, UK 8)

CUSHION PAD:
Round, 38cm (15in) diameter

OTHER ITEMS:
Plain round button with shank, 4cm (1½in) diameter
Tapestry needle

MEASUREMENTS:
40cm (16in) diameter, including ruffled border

Yarn Notes

This cushion has been made using Vivacious DK, a 100 per cent superwash merino wool from Fyberspates. The yarn is subtly space-dyed, resulting in a range of yellow tones. Any standard DK (8-ply) weight pure wool yarn could be used for this cushion, in a colour to suit your home decor.

Round 10: (2 tr in next st, 1 tr in each of next 9 sts) 12 times (132 sts); do not join to 1st st of round but continue working in a spiral.

Round 11: 1 tr in each st to end of round; do not join to 1st st of round but continue working in a spiral.

Round 12: 1 tr in each of next 11 sts, 1 htr in next st, 1 dc in next st, ss into next st; cut yarn and fasten off.

Ruffle

Select one of the circles to be the Front of the cushion.

Join yarn to stitch with marker at end of 1st round and proceed as follows, inserting hook into unworked front loop of each st and working in a spiral:

1 ch, (1 ss, 1 dc, 1 htr) in 1st st, (1 tr, 1 dtr) in next st, *3 dtr in next st, 2 dtr in next st, rep from * 19 times, then work 2 dtr in each st to end; fasten off.

Button cover

Foundation round: with 4.00mm (US G/6, UK 8) hook, make a magic ring and work 1 ch, 6 dc in ring; join with a ss to 1st dc of round (6 sts).

Round 1: 1 ch (does not count as a stitch), 2 dc in each dc of previous round; join with a ss to 1st dc of round (12 sts).

Round 2: 1 ch, 2 dc in each dc of previous round; join with a ss to 1st dc of round (24 sts).

Round 3: 1 ch, 1 dc in each dc of previous round; join with a ss to 1st dc of round.

Round 4: as round 3.

Round 5: 1 ch, 1 dc in 1st dc, (dc2tog over next 2 dc, 1 dc in next dc) seven times, dc2tog over last 2 dc; join with a ss to 1st dc of round (16 sts).

Cut yarn, leaving a tail, and fasten off.

Making up

Placing Front and Back of cushion right sides together, and join by slip stitching edges together, stitch by stitch. When seam is two-thirds complete, insert the cushion pad and continue joining the two edges; fasten off and weave in tails of yarn. For the covered button, thread the tail of yarn into a tapestry needle and pass the needle in and out of the stitch loops all around the edge of the Button Cover. Place the button inside the Button Cover and pull up the yarn tail to enclose the button; fasten off each yarn tail firmly, then stitch the button to the centre of the cushion Front.

The base of this cover is a crocheted circle with stitches worked into single loops. This leaves a spiral of unworked loops on the surface of the fabric, which form the foundation of the spiral ruffle.

A subtly variegated yarn helps to highlight the deeply textured ruffle and gives extra interest to the cover.

Peeking out of the centre of the ruffle is a co-ordinating covered button, which adds a neat finishing touch.

Ribbons

Textured stitches create three panels on the front of this pretty pillow, which are divided by two rows of eyelets threaded with velvet ribbons. This cushion is the perfect accessory for adding comfort and elegance to a bedroom or sitting room.

CUSHION PATTERN

The front of this cushion cover is worked in two textured patterns: at either end there is a cluster stitch and in the centre a ridged stitch, which is created by working some stitches around the post of a stitch two rows below. Each of the three textured panels is separated with a row of eyelets through which you can thread ribbon for extra interest. The back of the cushion is crocheted in rows of double crochet and is made up of two sections with an overlap, so that the cushion pad can be removed.

Tension

21 sts and 19 rows to 10cm (4in), measured over rows of dc using 4.00mm (US G/6, UK 8) hook and the recommended yarn.

Front

Foundation chain: with 4.00mm (US G/6, UK 8) hook, make 44 ch.

Foundation row (WS): 1 tr into 4th ch from hook, *miss 1 ch, (1 dc, 1 tr) in next ch; rep from * to last 2 ch, miss 1 ch, 1 dc in last ch; turn (41 sts).

Pattern 1

Row 1: 1 ch (counts as 1 dc), 1 tr in same place, * miss 1 tr, (1 dc, 1 tr) in next dc; rep from * to last 2 sts, miss 1 tr, 1 dc in top of turning ch; turn.

Rep row 1 seven times.

Eyelets

Row 1: 1 ch (does not count as a st), 1 dc in each st of previous row; turn.

Row 2: 4 ch (counts as 1 tr, 1 ch), *miss next st, 1 tr in next st, 1 ch; rep from * to end of row, 1 tr in top of turning ch; turn.

Row 3: 3 ch (counts as 1 tr), *1 tr into ch-sp, 1 tr in next tr; rep from * to end, working last tr into 3rd of 4 ch; turn.

Pattern 2

Row 1: 3 ch (counts as 1 tr), 1 tr in next tr, 1 tr in each rem st of previous row; turn.

Row 2: 3 ch, 1 tr in next tr, 1 dtr round post of tr below next tr, *1 tr in each of next 3 tr, 1 dtr round post of tr below next tr; rep from * to last 2 sts, 1 tr in each of last 2 sts; turn.

Row 3: 3 ch, 1 tr in next tr, 1 tr in each rem st of previous row.

EQUIPMENT

YARN:
Pure superwash merino wool DK (8-ply) yarn 2 x 115g (4oz) hanks in variegated pinks

HOOK:
4.00mm (US G/6, UK 8)

CUSHION PAD:
Rectangular, 40 x 25cm (16 x 10in)

OTHER ITEMS:
1.4m (4½ft) velvet ribbon, 1cm (½in) wide
Tapestry needle
Sewing thread to match yarn or ribbon

MEASUREMENTS:
40 x 25cm (16 x 10in)

Yarn Notes

This cushion has been made using Vivacious DK, a 100 per cent superwash merino wool from Fyberspates. The yarn is space-dyed, which results in its range of subtle berry tones. Any standard DK (8-ply) weight pure wool yarn could be used to make this cushion, in a colour to suit your home decor.

Row 4: 3 ch, *1 tr in each of next 3 tr, 1 tr round post of tr below next tr; rep from * to last 4 sts, 1 tr in each of last 4 sts; turn.

Row 5: as row 3.

Rep rows 2–5 twice more.

Eyelets

Row 1: 1 ch (does not count as a st), 1 dc in each st of previous row; turn.

Row 2: 4 ch (counts as 1 tr, 1 ch), *miss next st, 1 tr in next st, 1 ch; rep from * to end of row, 1 tr in top of turning ch; turn.

Row 3: 1 ch, *1 dc into ch-sp, 1 dc in next tr; rep from * to end, working last dc into 3rd of 4 ch; turn.

Rep row 1 of Pattern 1 nine times.

Cut yarn and fasten off.

Back (make two)

Foundation chain: with 4.00mm (US G/6, UK 8) hook, make 42 ch.

Foundation row: 1 dc in 2nd ch from hook, 1 dc in each ch to end (41 sts).

Row 1: 1 ch (does not counts as a st), 1 dc in each dc of previous row.

Rep row 1 33 times.

Cut yarn and fasten off.

Making up

With right sides facing out, line up the foundation edge of one of the Back pieces with the foundation edge of the Front and join by oversewing or with a flat seam (see pages 15 and 16). Do the same with the last row of the other Back piece and the last row of the Front. You will now have one long piece. Place this right side up on your work surface and fold the first piece along the seam, so that it is wrong side up, then fold the second Back piece along the seam, so that it lies on top of it, and the two Back pieces overlap. Pin the side seams together, then stitch, using matching yarn and backstitch.

Threading the ribbon

Cut the ribbon into four equal lengths. Beginning in the centre of one of the eyelet rows, thread a piece of ribbon in and out of the holes, from the centre to one edge, take the end through to the wrong side and secure the end to the side seam with a few small stitches. Repeat with the other three pieces of ribbon. Where the two ends emerge in the centre of each eyelet row, tie them in a neat bow. Turn the cushion cover right sides out and insert the cushion pad.

Combining stitch patterns makes this project interesting to crochet and produces a cover that looks and feels lovely.

Choose velvet ribbon that is the same width as the eyelets and in a colour
that makes a pleasing contrast with the yarn. Secure the ends of the ribbons
in the seams.

The central section of the cover is formed
of rows of trebles; some of the stitches are
worked around the post of the stitch in the
row below, instead of into the top of the
stitch, creating a pleasing ridged texture.

Luxury

This long, firm cushion is perfect for a bedroom or dressing room. Use a luxury yarn for the front of the cushion and the same for the back, if you are feeling extravagant. Or you can choose to use a less expensive yarn for the back of the cushion, if you prefer – just make sure it has the same tension.

CUSHION PATTERN

This cushion is simply worked in rows of double crochet, with a contrast double crochet seam creating a border all round.

Tension

17 sts and 21 rows to 10cm (4in), measured over rows of dc using a 4.00mm (US G/6, UK 8) hook and the recommended yarn.

Front

Foundation chain: with 4.00mm (US G/6, UK 8) hook and yarn A, make 47 ch.

Foundation row (RS): 1 dc in 2nd ch from hook, 1 dc in each ch to end; turn (46 sts).

Row 1: 1 ch (does not count as st), 1 dc in each dc of previous row; turn.

Rep row 1 112 times more; do not turn after end of last row but work 100 dc along side edge, 1 dc in each of 46 ch on short edge and 100 dc along opposite side.

Cut yarn and fasten off.

Back

Follow instructions for Front.

Button borders (make three)

Foundation round: using 3.50mm (US E/4, UK 9) hook and yarn B, make a magic ring and work 1 ch (does not count as a st), 6 dc into ring; join with a ss in 1st dc of round (6 sts).

Round 1: 1 ch, 2 dc in each dc of previous round; join with a ss in 1st dc of round (12 sts).

Round 2: 1 ch, 2 dc in each dc of previous round; join with a ss in 1st dc of round (24 sts).

Cut yarn, leaving a tail, and fasten off.

EQUIPMENT

YARN:

Luxury lambswool–mohair yarn, 4 x 50g (1¾oz) balls in pale pink (A), and metallised fine 3-ply yarn, 1 x 25g (1oz) ball in metallic silver (B)

HOOK:

4.00mm (US G/6, UK 8) and 3.50mm (US E/4, UK 9)

CUSHION PAD:

Rectangular, 55 x 30cm (22 x 12in)

OTHER ITEMS:

Tapestry needle

3 fancy buttons, 25mm (1in) diameter

Upholsterer's needle or long sharp darning needle

Strong thread

MEASUREMENTS:

53 x 28cm (21¼ x 11in)

Yarn Notes

This cushion has been made using Rowan Kid Classic, a luxurious blend of lambswool and kid mohair. There are 140m (153 yds) in a 50g (1¾oz) ball. The border and embellishments are crocheted in Twilley's Goldfingering, a blend of 80 per cent viscose and 20 per cent metallised polyester. There are 100m (110 yds) in a 25g (1oz) ball. DMC Lumina is a metallic yarn with a similar composition but with 150m (164 yds) in a 20g (¾oz) ball.

Making up

Place the two pieces together, right sides out, lining up the edges. With 3.50mm (US E/4, UK 9) hook and yarn B, join, stitch by stitch, with dc, inserting the hook into one loop only of each dc on both edges. Leave an opening on one of the short edges and insert the cushion pad, then continue joining the two edges; fasten off and weave in tails of yarn.

Attaching the buttons

Pin the three Button Borders, evenly spaced, to the front of the cushion. Using tails of yarn and a tapestry needle, stitch each one in place. Thread an upholsterer's needle or long sharp needle with strong thread and fasten the thread to the centre of one of the crocheted circles, then take the needle right through the cushion at this point and back through to the front, then through the shank of one of the buttons and back through the cushion at the same point. Pull tightly on the thread to create a dimple in the cushion, take the needle back through the cushion and through the button shank, then fasten off the thread securely behind the button. Repeat for the other two buttons (see top tip box).

TOP TIP

Use an upholsterer's needle or a very long darning needle with a sharp point to penetrate right through the cushion pad, and pull the thread very tightly, knotting it firmly, to create the desired dimpled effect.

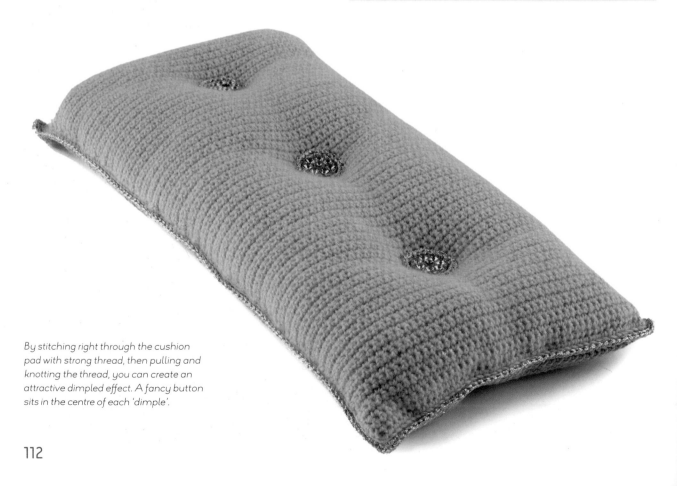

By stitching right through the cushion pad with strong thread, then pulling and knotting the thread, you can create an attractive dimpled effect. A fancy button sits in the centre of each 'dimple'.

Try to find some fancy buttons to add the right decorative detail. These came from a little shop that sells sari fabrics. Each button sits in the centre of a crocheted circle made from glittery yarn, enhancing the sparkly effect.

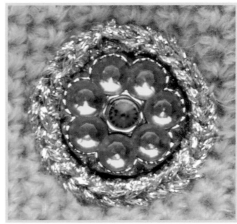

A long, narrow, firm cushion is ideal for the end of a couch or chaise longue, or to dress up a bed. To create the right degree of firmness, choose a pad that is slightly larger than the cover but not so large that it stretches and distorts the crocheted fabric.

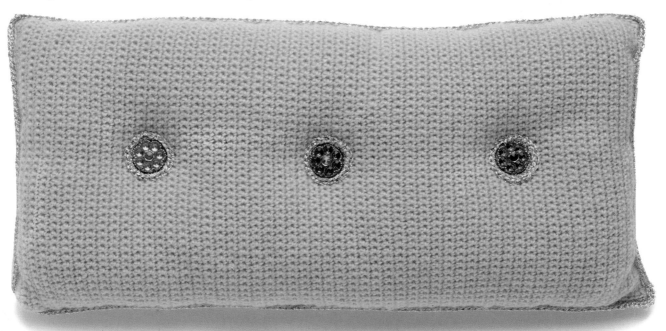

Pincushion

The perfect gift for a needlecrafter, this practical little cushion, crocheted from fine cotton and stuffed firmly, could do double duty as a doll-sized footstool. Choose your own colour scheme – it's a great project for using up leftover yarn.

CUSHION PATTERN

This cushion is worked in rounds of double crochet.

Tension

Work a tension sample to the end of round 6, using 2.50mm (US B/1 or C/2, UK 12) hook and recommended yarn; this should measure 7.5cm (3in) in diameter.

Top

Foundation round: with 2.50mm (US B/1 or C/2, UK 12) hook and yarn A, make a magic ring and work 1 ch (does not count as st), 6 dc into ring; join with a ss to 1st dc (6 sts).

Round 1: 1 ch, 2 dc in each dc of previous round (12 sts).

Round 2: 1 ch, 1 dc in 1st dc, (3 dc in next dc, 1 dc in next dc) five times, 3 dc in last dc; join with a ss to 1st dc of round; joining in yarn B as you do so; do not cut yarn A (24 sts).

Round 3: with yarn B, 1 ch, 1 dc in each dc to end of round; join with a ss to 1st dc of round.

Round 4: 1 ch, 1 dc in 1st dc, 1 dc in next dc, (3 dc in next dc, 1 dc in each of next 3 dc) five times, 3 dc in next dc, 1 dc in next dc; join with a ss to 1st dc of round (36 sts).

Round 5: with yarn A, 1 ch, 1 dc in each dc to end of round; join with a ss to 1st dc of round.

Round 6: 1 ch, 1 dc in 1st dc, 1 dc in each of next 2 dc, (3 dc in next dc, 1 dc in each of next 5 dc) five times, 3 dc in next dc, 1 dc in each of next 2 dc; join with a ss to 1st dc of round (48 sts).

Round 7: with yarn B, 1 ch, 1 dc in each dc to end of round; join with a ss to 1st dc of round.

Round 8: 1 ch, 1 dc in 1st dc, 1 dc in each of next 3 dc, (3 dc in next dc, 1 dc in each of next 7 dc) five times, 3 dc in next dc, 1 dc in each of next 3 dc; join with a ss to 1st dc of round (60 sts).

Round 9: with yarn A, 1 ch, 1 dc in each dc to end of round; join with a ss to 1st dc of round.

Round 10: 1 ch, 1 dc in 1st dc, 1 dc in each of next 4 dc, (3 dc in next dc, 1 dc in each of next 9 dc) five times, 3 dc in next dc, 1 dc in each of next 4 dc; join with a ss to 1st dc of round (72 sts).

EQUIPMENT

YARN:

Fingering (4-ply) cotton yarn, 1 x 100g (3½oz) ball each in bright pink (A) and green (B)

HOOK:

2.50mm (US B/1 or C/2, UK 12)

CUSHION FILLING:

Polyester toy filling

MEASUREMENTS:

10cm (4in) diameter and 4cm (1½in) deep

Yarn Notes

This cushion has been made using Patons 100 per cent Cotton 4-ply, a silky smooth, tightly spun mercerised cotton available in a good range of vibrant colours. There are 330m (360 yds) in a 100g (3½oz) ball. If you decide to substitute another yarn, a 50g (1¾oz) ball of each colour will be sufficient.

Round 11: with yarn B, 1 ch, 1 dc in each dc to end of round; join with a ss to 1st dc of round.

Round 12: 1 ch, 1 dc in 1st dc, 1 dc in each of next 5 dc, (3 dc in next dc, 1 dc in each of next 11 dc) five times, 3 dc in next dc, 1 dc in each of next 5 dc; join with a ss to 1st dc of round (84 sts).

Cut yarn and fasten off.

Base

Follow the instructions for the Top to the end of round 12; fasten off yarn B and continue in yarn A as follows to create the sides:

Round 1: inserting the hook into the back loop only of each st (for this round only), work 1 ch, 1 dc in each dc to end of round.

Round 2: 1 ch, 1 dc in each dc of previous round.

Rep round 2 eight times.

Do not cut yarn but join to edge of Top with a double crochet seam (see page 17), inserting the hook into one loop only on each edge. Before completing the round, insert stuffing, then close gap.

Making up

There are no separate making-up instructions, as the Sides are worked upwards from the Base then joined to the Top, as described in the pattern instructions above.

Making six increases on every other round forms a distinctive hexagonal pattern. Choose your own combination of colours; this cushion is very small, making it ideal for using up leftover yarn.

Working rounds of double crochet without increases forms a neat gusset all round, giving the cushion depth.

For a practical pincushion, you need to create a firm fabric – and a smooth, tightly twisted cotton yarn is ideal for this. You should be able to stuff it quite firmly without stretching it out of shape.

Wedding

This dainty little lace cushion is designed to be used as a ring pillow in a wedding ceremony, carried by one of the bridesmaids or perhaps a pageboy. Tie the rings in place using satin ribbon bows.

CUSHION PATTERN

This cushion is crocheted in the round, starting with a round motif, which becomes a square. The ruffle border with picot edge is added after the back and front of the cushion cover have been joined together.

Tension

Using the recommended yarn and a 3.75mm (US F/5, UK 8 or 9) hook, the central square (up to the end of round 6) measures 13cm (5in).

Front

Foundation chain: with 3.75mm (US F/5, UK 8 or 9) hook and yarn, make a magic ring and work 1 ch, 8 dc into ring; join with a ss to 1st dc (8 sts).

Round 1: 3 ch (counts as 1 tr), 1 tr in same place, 2 tr in each dc to end of round; join with a ss to 3rd of 3 ch (16 sts).

Round 2: 4 ch (counts as 1 tr, 1 ch), (1 tr in next tr, 1 ch) 15 times; join with a ss in 3rd of 4 ch.

Round 3: ss into 1st 1-ch sp, 1 ch (counts as 1 dc), 1 dc in same 1-ch sp, 3 ch, 2 dc in next 1-ch sp, 3 ch) 15 times; join with a ss into 1 ch.

Round 4: ss into 1st 3-ch sp, 4 ch (counts as 1 dc, 3 ch), (1 dc in next 3-ch sp, 3 ch) 15 times; join with a ss into 1st of 3 ch.

Round 5: 1 ch, * 4 ch, miss next 3-ch sp (dtr cluster, 5 ch, dtr cluster) in next 3-ch sp, 4 ch, miss next 3-ch sp, 1 dc in next dc, 5 ch, miss next 3-ch sp, 1 dc in next dc; rep from * three times more, working last dc into 1st of 5 ch.

Round 6: ss into 1st 4-ch sp, 4 ch (counts as 1 tr, 1 ch), 1 tr in same sp, 1 ch, *(1 tr, 1 ch, 1 tr, 3 ch, 1 tr, 1 ch, 1 tr) in next 5-ch sp, 1 ch, (1 tr, 1 ch) twice in each of next 3 spaces; rep from * twice more, (1 tr, 1 ch, 1 tr, 3 ch, 1 tr, 1 ch, 1 tr) in next 5-ch sp, 1 ch, (1 tr, 1 ch) twice in each of next 2 spaces; join with a ss into 3rd of 4 ch.

Round 7: ss into 1st 1-ch sp, 4 ch, (1 tr in next sp, 1 ch) twice, *(1 tr, 1 ch, 1 tr, 3 ch, 1 tr, 1 ch, 1 tr, 1 ch) in corner sp, (1 tr in next sp, 1 ch) nine times; rep from * twice, (1 tr, 1 ch, 1 tr, 3 ch, 1 tr, 1 ch, 1 tr, 1 ch) in corner sp, (1 tr in next sp, 1 ch) six times; join with a ss into 3rd of 4 ch.

Round 8: ss into 1st 1-ch sp, 4 ch, (1 tr in next sp, 1 ch) three times, *(1 tr, 1 ch, 1 tr, 3 ch, 1 tr, 1 ch, 1 tr, 1 ch) in corner sp, (1 tr in next sp, 1 ch) 12 times; rep from * twice, (1 tr, 1 ch, 1 tr, 3 ch, 1 tr, 1 ch, 1 tr, 1 ch) in corner sp, (1 tr in next sp, 1 ch) eight times; join with a ss into 3rd of 4 ch.

EQUIPMENT

YARN:
Wool–cashmere blend light DK (8-ply) yarn, 2 x 50g (1¾oz) balls in white

HOOK:
3.75mm (US F/5, UK 8 or 9)

CUSHION PAD:
Square, 23 x 23cm (9½ x 9½in), covered with cotton fabric in blue or other pastel colour

OTHER ITEMS:
60cm (24in) pink satin ribbon, 6mm (¼in) wide (optional)
60cm (24in) ivory satin ribbon, 3mm (⅛in) wide (optional)

MEASUREMENTS:
26 x 26cm (10½ x 10½in), including border

Yarn Notes

This cushion is made from Debbie Bliss Baby Cashmerino, a blend of 55 per cent merino wool, 33 per cent acrylic and 12 per cent cashmere, making it soft and luxurious but also very practical. There are 125m (137 yds) in a 50g (1¾oz) ball. There are a number of similar yarns on the market. This one is lighter than a standard DK (8-ply) yarn but thicker than a fingering (4-ply), so if you do substitute another yarn, be sure to check the tension or your cushion cover may turn out smaller or larger than the one shown, and you will need a different sized cushion pad.

Round 9: ss into 1st 1-ch sp, 4 ch, (1 tr in next sp, 1 ch) four times, *(1 tr, 1 ch, 1 tr, 3 ch, 1 tr, 1 ch, 1 tr, 1 ch) in corner sp, (1 tr in next sp, 1 ch) 15 times; rep from * twice, (1 tr, 1 ch, 1 tr, 3 ch, 1 tr, 1 ch, 1 tr, 1 ch) in corner sp, (1 tr in next sp, 1 ch) 10 times; join with a ss into 3rd of 4 ch.

Round 10: ss into 1st 1-ch sp, 4 ch, (1 tr in next sp, 1 ch) five times, *(1 tr, 1 ch, 1 tr, 3 ch, 1 tr, 1 ch, 1 tr, 1 ch) in corner sp, (1 tr in next sp, 1 ch) 18 times; rep from * twice, (1 tr, 1 ch, 1 tr, 3 ch, 1 tr, 1 ch, 1 tr, 1 ch) in corner sp, (1 tr in next sp, 1 ch) 12 times; join with a ss into 3rd of 4 ch.

Round 11: 1 ch (does not count as a st), 1 dc in same place, then 1 dc in each tr and ch-sp of previous round, except (2 dc, 1 htr, 2 dc) in each corner st (200 sts).

Cut yarn and fasten off.

Back

Follow instructions for Front but do not cut yarn after completing round 11.

Making up and border

To join the cushion cover, place Back and Front together, right sides out and using the same yarn work a row of dc all round, inserting hook through one loop only of each corresponding edge stitch on both pieces, creating a neat raised seam (see page 17). When seam is three-quarters complete, insert the cushion pad and continue joining the two edges, then create the frilled edge as follows:

Round 1: 3 ch (counts as 1 tr), 1 tr in same place, 2 tr in each dc of previous round; join with a ss to 3rd of 3 ch (400 sts).

Round 2: 1 ch (does not count as a st), 1 dc in same place, 3 ch, 1 dc in next st, *1 dc in next st, 3 ch, 1 dc in next st; rep from * to end of round; join with a ss to 1st dc.

Cut yarn and fasten off. See top tip box, below.

Note:

As this cushion cover has holes, you will be able to see the cushion pad underneath, so make a simple fabric cover in a contrasting colour, using pale blue cotton, as in the cushion pictured here, or in your choice of colour.

TOP TIP

Working two or more stitches into one, all round the edge of the cushion, creates a ruffled border that is easy to achieve and very effective. Here two trebles are worked into each double crochet of the perimeter seam. A similar technique is used to create the ruffled effect for the cushion on page 102.

Slip lengths of narrow satin ribbon under the stitch loops at two opposite corners of the central motif: these can be used to tie wedding rings in place.

Show the eyelet lace pattern to best effect by covering the cushion pad in a contrasting colour.

The richly ruffled border is simply created by working pairs of trebles into each stitch around the outer edge of the cushion.

House

This little novelty cushion would make a good housewarming present. It can be used as an accent cushion, and the diminutive size and rectangular shape also make it very practical as a kneeler or to tuck behind you when sitting in a chair, to help support the small of your back.

CUSHION PATTERN

This cushion is worked in rows of double crochet. The colourwork details are worked following a chart, see below, and using the intarsia method. Each coloured square on the chart represents a stitch. Each colour change is done in the last stage of the previous stitch. Colours not in use are carried at the back of the work. Where there is a large block of colour (more than three stitches in a row), it is advisable to use a separate length of yarn, wound on to a bobbin, to prevent too much stranding.

Intarsia colour chart.

EQUIPMENT

YARN:

100 per cent extra fine merino wool superwash DK (8-ply) yarn, 2 x 50g (1¾oz) balls in pale blue (A) and 1 x 50g (1¾oz) ball each in teal (B), pink (C) and white (D)

HOOK:

3.75mm (US F/5, UK 8 or 9)

CUSHION PAD:

Rectangular, 30 x 15cm (12 x 6in)

OTHER ITEMS:

Tapestry needle

MEASUREMENTS:

32 x 17cm (12¾ x 6¾in)

Yarn Notes

A soft pure wool yarn is ideal for this little cushion, which has been made using Debbie Bliss Rialto, spun from 100 per cent extra fine merino wool, chosen for its softness and for the wide choice of subtle colours. There are 105m (115 yds) in a 50g (1¾oz) ball. You could choose to substitute another standard DK (8-ply) weight yarn and, of course, choose your own palette of four colours.

Tension

20 sts and 22 rows to 10cm (4in), measured over rows of dc using 3.75mm (US F/5, UK 8 or 9) hook and the recommended yarn.

Back

Foundation chain: with 3.75mm (US F/5, UK 8 or 9) hook and yarn A, make 35 ch.

Foundation row (RS): 1 dc in 2nd ch from hook, 1 dc in each ch to end (34 sts).

Row 1: 1 ch (does not count as st), 1 dc in each dc of previous row.

Rep row 1 50 times more; cut A and join in B.

Using B, rep row 1 nine times more.

Next row: 1 ch, inserting hook into back loop only of each st (for this row only), 1 dc in each dc of previous row.

Rep row 1 nine times more.

Next row (picots): *3 ch, ss into each of next 2 sts; rep from * to last st, 3 ch, ss in last st.

Front

Foundation chain: with 3.75mm (US F/5, UK 8 or 9) hook and yarn A, make 35 ch.

Foundation row (RS): 1 dc in 2nd ch from hook, 1 dc in each ch to end (34 sts).

Row 1: 1 ch (does not count as st), 1 dc in each dc of previous row.

Continue, following the chart on page 122 from row 3 onwards.

Sewing the windows

Thread a tapestry needle with a length of yarn B and stitch lines vertically and horizontally on each window, in backstitch, to represent the frame (see top tip box).

Making up

With right sides out, join the foundation row on Back and Front by oversewing or using the flat seam method (see page 16). Fold across this seam, so that right sides are together, lining up the side edges. Stitch side seams in backstitch (see page 14). Turn right sides out and insert cushion pad, then fold roof flap to front and backstitch along base of picot edge. If you wish to be able to remove the cushion pad, you may prefer to attach press fasteners along the edge of the roofline instead, or simply leave the roof flap unattached.

A row of picots worked into the edge of the roof forms a textured ridge when the roof is stitched in place.

Work the window shape using the intarsia method on page 122, then embroider the window bars in backstitch.

The roof is formed by a flap: you can choose to stitch this down, after inserting the cushion pad, or leave it open so that the cushion cover can double as a pyjama case.

Reference

Tension (gauge)

Check your tension before you start crocheting your cushion cover, to make sure it ends up the right size. To check if your tension is correct, work a swatch using the specified yarn and hook, then measure it using a ruler (rather than a tape measure) to count the number of stitches and rows over 10cm (4in). If you have more stitches and rows than the number stated in the pattern, this indicates that you work more tightly than the stated tension and your finished item is likely to end up too small, so you will have to try again using a larger hook. If you have fewer stitches, you tend to crochet more loosely, so try again with a smaller hook until you achieve the correct tension. For some patterns in the book, the tension is measured over dc, rather than the given stitch in the project: it is sometimes easier to do a quick double-crochet sample, rather than a sample over the pattern stitch. If the dc sample is the right tension, it should follow that the tension will also be correct over pattern.

Hook conversions

Metric	US	UK
2.5mm	B/1 or C/2	12
3.0mm	C/2 or D/3	11
3.5mm	E/4	9
3.75mm	F/5	8 or 9
4.0mm	G/6	8
4.5mm	7	7
5.0mm	H/8	6
8.0mm	L/11	0

Yarn conversions

US	UK	Australia
worsted	aran	10-ply
DK or light worsted	DK or 8-ply	8-ply
fingering	4-ply	4-ply

Abbreviations

beg	begin(ning)
st	stitch
ss	slipstitch
ch	chain
dc	double crochet
htr	half treble
tr	treble
dtr	double treble
rep	repeat
RS	right side
WS	wrong side
dc2tog	work 2 double crochet together over next two stitches

UK–US crochet term conversions

This book uses standard UK crochet terms throughout, but here is a useful chart showing UK–US crochet term conversions. The same terms are sometimes used for different stitches, so it is worth being aware of this.

UK	US
double crochet (dc)	single crochet (sc)
treble (tr)	double crochet (dc)
half treble (htr)	half double crochet (hdc)
double treble (dtr)	treble crochet (tr)

Ball-shaped template

For a ball cushion 50cm (20in) in diameter, like the one used on pages 30–33, enlarge this pattern piece so that it measures 160cm (5¼ft) from point to point. Allowing about 1.5cm (½in) for seam allowances, when you join eight pieces together you will have a ball with a diameter of 50cm (20in) and a circumference of 157cm (5ft).

Index

Acknowledgements

Thank you to Becky Shackleton for her patience and expertise in editing and co-ordinating this book and to Paul Bricknell and Laura Forrester for their photography, which shows the finished cushions to their best advantage. Thanks also to Coats, Rowan, Sirdar, King Cole, Designer Yarns, DMC and Sublime for providing me with the yarns used to develop and make the finished cushion covers.